Love Tails
True animal stories to inspire & uplift
Kye Crow

Love Tails

www.kyecrow.love

First Published 2024

Love Tails is also available as an e-book

When you enter the realms

of the

animals with no

desire to profit or gain,

something extraordinary happens

that few get to share.

Contents

One

Our Fairy Herd

We have a ritual here each morning that has become our dawn chorus. It begins at first light as I am lying in bed when I hear the faraway sound of galloping feet. It's the percussive beat of our herd of horses galloping in from the paddock next door. As they get close, the sound of their fast-moving hooves builds to a thrilling crescendo. One by one, they pass my window-from tiny mini ponies to big stocky horses; more often than not, a mini pony is leading, and I love how our big horses can run in their midst, always adjusting their pace so they don't run over their little mates.

Sometimes, when the earth is dry, they arrive in a cloud of dust and in winter, I have seen them galloping in through the mist as the sun rose behind them. It's always a phenomenal and breathtaking experience that leaves every cell in my body zinging with life. Gill has a deep connection with the horses and shared that the sound of their galloping feet releases trauma from our earth. That may be why there is such a deep peace around them.

After their dramatic entrance, they settle under a tree for a sleep- yes, that's right, they come at the speed of light for a slumber party right outside our home.

Many days, we watch them happily while feeding our huge tribe of hungry animals or carting hay down to our other horses that may be in recovery and have yet to join the herd.

Some mornings, we go and slip in among this herd. Our bums in the dirt as we sit, revelling in the love-filled and peaceful emanations of our horses. It is so easy to believe in the goodness and magic of life when you are with them.

We have all sorts of rescued horses, from tiny miniature ponies to ex-trotters and old breeding mares. When the first big horses arrived, I worried they would harm the little ones. A senseless worry I see now. I never thought they would be aggressive, only that the natural shenanigans between horses would disadvantage our little mini ponies.

When the mini ponies first came, they were with a big guardian horse, an ex-trotter called Spirit.

I had seen a call for help for them in a rescue group on social media. Spirit and five mini ponies needed a home as their owner could not afford to feed them. The country was in drought, hay prices were soaring, yet even so, I felt this wee herd was meant to come to us. I commented on the post and offered them all home. They could stay together if they all came to us, but my offer was refused. I was told they had already found homes. When I read through the comments, I was shocked. One person wanted the pretty white one; another would take the trotter, and someone else thought the silver taffy shetland would be great for their kids. I could not believe that a rescue organisation would choose to separate friends when they had an offer to keep them all together.

I have always wanted a giant wolfhound but never got one because there has always been some other needy dog. It's not about whether an animal is pretty or what I want; I rescue and help animals-full stop. I am not fulfilling my personal desires to own or obtain specific animals. I found their attitude deeply disappointing, but there was nothing I could do. I *had* to let go.

I love it when we can keep animal friends together; I wish more people understood that animals are just like us and forge bonds of love that cause them trauma when they are separated.

A few days later, I saw the post again- *maybe the homes had all fallen through*. I felt a surge of elation. Yes, this beautiful tribe would get to stay together. So I offered once more, but again, I was refused, this time a little curtly. *We have already told you they have homes!* I was even beginning to wonder if it was personal but once again there was nothing I could do. *Why had I felt so strongly they were meant to come to us?* I let go - *again.*

Within a few days, I noticed they were being advertised again, but this time, there was a location. We live remote, over a thousand kilometres inland, far away from the madding crowd. This wee tribe of ponies lived in the closest town to us, seventy-five kilometres away. While we had been prepared to do the hard miles to go and pick them up, it appeared that none who'd offered them homes were. I couldn't believe it; I had not known their location and presumed we would have a long journey to get them. I offered again, and this time, I was accepted. Did I notice a morsel of contriteness in their humble acceptance of our offer? I thought so, but I didn't care. These horses were finally coming to us, which made me very happy.

We bought them home in two lots. First, we picked up the ex-trotter Spirit and the silver shetland. They spent the first night here on their own, calling out frantically for their friends. They were really missing them, and I couldn't wait to reunite them the following day. When we finally got the others back, before we had even unloaded them, they were whinnying to Spirit and the shetland pony we eventually called Taffy. The excitement and joy they all expressed when finally reunited was so beautiful it had me in tears. I know there are times when animals have to be separated to find them homes, but surely we should turn over every stone and give priority to anyone offering to honour these bonds of love and affection.

I loved these horses, they were like a fairy tribe and adored their big Spirit, he however was very aloof with us. I often see this in horses who have been worked, raced, trotted or ridden a lot before they came to us.

When you give a horse his life back and release him into a paddock so he is free to move across the land, sleep when he chooses, graze on a whim, with no expectation to work or perform or be of service again, they often move far away from even wanting human connection. All our horses with a riding or racing history have done this. I am aware, though, that many people are creating more conscious relationships with horses that are shifting the way they are ridden- bit-less bridles, animal connection and communication, building relationships that honour them and listen to their needs. All this is deeply encouraging, but here at our haven, nothing is expected of them.

When they first arrive, they are suspicious of us mere humans. They watch us in a guarded way, unwilling to share their holy treasure, the gift of who they are- yet. They are elusive and do not want to be touched. When we approach, they move away and won't come close. It's OK, we give them time. They have not experienced a human that did not seek gratification from them before.

As the days pass and they realise no one has come to saddle them up, no one has tried to harness them, they become more confident and more curious to know who we are. Then they hesitantly come towards us and give us a cautious whiff. This initial moment of connection feels like a sacred anointment, a well-earned blessing, but it's not a reward. The reward is seeing them live wild and free and in their power.

It took time to build a relationship with Spirit; those who had profited from him passed him from one person to the next and then discarded him when he no longer won a race. He had never thought highly of humans until now. Now he comes and stands by me, and we bathe in each other's energy as if we are dancing together in the purest light; I feel him, and he feels me; there is not always the need to touch.

Our big, beautiful Spirit has lived with us for almost six years. He is the one who reassures the new horses that they are OK. *Don't worry; it is freedom and love here. These humans walk in their own power and do not need yours*.

Last year, we had a hailstorm in the middle of the night. A million canon balls of ice hammered on the roof of our bus; when it had passed, Gill and I went outside to check our animals. The weight of the ice had torn awnings down and ripped the shade that sheltered our garden. Trees were down, and the ground was covered in so many leaves blown from the trees; even in our torchlight, the earth looked as if it was in a frenzy of spring.

While the animals around the home were all fine, we suddenly realised that many wild birds that hung out in our garden may not be. Over the years, we have come to know this tribe of apostle birds and knew they always slept in the same tree. With only the beam of a fast-fading torch, we ran to the tree and found so many of our feathered friends lying frozen on the ground as if dead. We gathered them all up, headed home, and spent the next hour drying them with a hair dryer. We had pet carriers, which were toasty and warm, with heat pads and electric blankets that allowed the birds to recover. We made several trips out that night, searching under other trees and finding parrots, crows, and many other little birds that had already perished. We thawed the survivors out and released them all the following day. It was beautiful watching all our feathered neighbours return to their trees.

The hail stones had had a catastrophic impact on so many birds, and the following day, the carnage in nature was everywhere. We had thought all our animals were OK until Spirit came home. One eye had gone completely blind, and we can only assume it was the hail. It wasn't like that before the storm, and while it's been two years since he lost his sight in that eye, it's not made any difference to him. He still gallops in each morning with his herd and still hangs out and cares for his mini friends, but these days, he is much more affable with me and loves nothing more than a good old cuddle.

Two

Boo & the Emu

I t was early in the morning. The galahs were squawking in the huge gum tree in our garden. We had just given our five orphaned joeys their bottle when our phone rang. It was one of our dear friends, a wildlife rescuer, who, like many others in our wildlife group, didn't only care for wildlife - they loved all animals.

'Kye, I have just heard a dog is running around near you that is badly injured. It's a small white fluffy dog, and it's with a big black one.'

Without a moment's hesitation, we jumped into the car, unaware that we were embarking on a treasure trail that would lead us to a precious gift.

We had yet to learn who the dogs belonged to, but it wasn't unusual for locals to ask us to help an animal in our community. There was a lot of drug and alcohol abuse, and sometimes animal welfare got missed. We had already rehomed a small male dog that had ended up badly injured by a larger male as they fought over a bitch in heat. A wonderful friend had taken him on, paid for his extensive vet bills, had him desexed and nursed him through his lengthy recovery. This little dog was so adored and pampered he had truly landed on his feet.

We had no idea what we would discover as we drove around the town, stopping periodically to ask a passer-by if they had seen these dogs. No one had, but each person told us of someone with dogs that matched the description. We knocked on numerous doors, waiting while people went to check to see if their dogs were at home, and they always were and none reported that they were injured.

After hours of searching, we were on the verge of returning home when we were told of yet another man who owned a small, fluffy white dog. By this time, I was exhausted, so I sat in the car waiting while Gill went in and asked. Ten minutes later, he came out carrying this gorgeous giant fluffy X wolfhound mastiff puppy. It was the most beautiful puppy I had ever seen.

'He couldn't afford to feed him, Kye; I had to get him.'

As I looked at this trembling dog, I could feel we had been given a phenomenal treasure. One that surpassed diamonds or jewels, or beautiful cars or any of those false and illusory rewards that so many prize. A treasure that only the wise and those who lived from their hearts would recognise.

Gill told me the puppy had been living in a tiny yard that didn't even have a bush to offer shade from the sun's heat. A dead chicken was lying in the dirt, and rubbish was scattered everywhere. We had no idea if this pup had killed the chicken, but I was not unduly worried even though we had many chickens. I had witnessed many dogs, no matter their age, leave their killing ways behind when they came to live with us. This dog was still young, so we had plenty of time to teach him new ways. But beyond superficial concerns, so much more was going on within me. I felt as if I had reunited with an old and much-loved friend, and I knew the trail we had followed that morning had never been about finding a little fluffy white dog; it had led to this phenomenal creature who looked as if he had stepped straight out of the pages of a fairy tale. From the moment I saw him, I felt this immense love for this scruffy wild looking dog.

'You're gonna be ok', I said reassuringly, and as I did, he reached over to me and gave me a gentle lick. He was still nervous and unsure, but I knew it wouldn't take him long to see his life had just bloomed.

And this was how Boo, our wonderful guardian and protector, came into our lives. We went out searching for one dog and came home with another, and despite coming from a long line of dogs bred specifically for pig hunting, he became our intelligent and gentle giant.

Over the years, we witnessed him comfort many animals on the edge of death, malnourished and weak. Animals felt innately safe with him; he slept with the chickens, and even our galah parrot Pops, whom we had freed from decades in a cage, would perch on him and preen himself.

Boo always offered the perfect response to an animal's needs. Once, I had driven fifty kilometres- halfway to town to meet a friend with an orphaned newborn lamb on the very edge of death. Boo had been with me, and on the drive home, he sat in the back, snuggling up to this babe, giving it much-needed body heat and attention as I raced home. I prayed it would survive, but I was not hopeful. It was barely conscious when we picked it up, so I was overjoyed to see this lamb lift his little head when we finally got home. I am sure Boo played a significant part in this baby animal's return to life. He was a nursemaid and a guardian, though the latter was more due to his intimidating size. However, one morning, he showed us he was indeed our guardian angel and protector.

We always went for a pre-breakfast walk around the edge of the lake, and it wasn't only our dogs that loved this daily routine. There would be a whole gaggle of animals coming along. Our goat Powpow would follow, as would Bella our donkey, and Oochi, our wee mini pony. Our pigs, Sweetheart, Tuppy and Pumpkin, loved the daily walks; they got to scoff down any new shoots they discovered along the way and wallow in the lake's muddy shores. Flying beside us would be a variety of parrots, usually Hank, who had lived in a tiny cage at a pub for several decades and been taught by the locals a colourful range of swear words. Despite his new life living freely in a place of love, we had never been able to curb his swearing and often had to warn people who visited our sanctuary to block their ears, especially if they had children. Sometimes, kangaroos we'd hand-reared but already released would hop along with us as well. We were always a colourful procession of people and animals, and I loved how so many different species of animals got on. However, some could be a little cheeky-especially our hand-reared emus.

We had just reached the edge of the lake when we saw a group of emus in the distance. Over the years, we'd hand-reared many orphaned emus. Some still hung around home, several had returned to the wild but would still, occasionally, come and say hello if they saw us on a walk. I loved seeing them and witnessing how they had integrated back into the wild.

If you have not hand-reared an orphan emu, you may be unaware of their temperaments. Emus are one of my favourite creatures to hand rear. I love them; they are incredibly affectionate creatures, but they also have this wild, flamboyant side and can get really excited. I often think they resemble a tribal witch doctor performing some ancient ceremony. All their feathers stand up; they throw themselves on the ground and then leap high into the air before taking off at a run, moving in a zig-zag. Then, they throw themselves on the ground again and repeat their entire performance. They are hilarious to watch, especially when several are doing this wild dance simultaneously.

As the group of emus got closer, we could tell one of them was ours. The first emu we had ever reared whom we had barely seen since he'd returned as an adult to the wild. I was relieved to see him living with the wild emus. I worried when I didn't see them. When you hand-rear an orphan animal or a bird from being tiny and do everything you can to help them return to the wild, it's a gift to see the living proof that you succeeded. I was delighted to see Zeb, though unprepared for his utter excitement at seeing us. He was elated.

He began running wildly right through the middle of our entourage and was frightening our dogs as well as our new staghound Chez, who, if she had seen an emu before, hadn't seen a mad one like this. All our animals were scattering in different directions. I was rushing to try and gather up our two tiny dogs, Rosy and Meerzi, who were running away from us in a panic. While Zeb was a hand-reared emu, it is always wise to be extremely cautious with them. They do have the potential to be dangerous, even if that is not their intention. I was alarmed; in all the turmoil, I had not been able to catch our little dogs, and one of them was running in a panic towards Zeb. I had no idea what to do. I should have known we would be looked after, but in all the madness, I could never have anticipated how help would come. And, of course, it came from our wise and loving protector, Boo.

Boo knew exactly what needed to be done and responded swiftly when he saw little Meerzi was in the direct line of Zeb's deadly clawed feet. He ran between Meerzi and Zeb and began barking at Zeb to get his attention, distracting our excited emu so I could run in and grab our little frightened dog. With our little dogs safely in our arms, we watched Boo take off at a run, heading away from us into the open field with Zeb hot on his heels.

The fun Boo and Zeb were having as they ran in big circles chasing each other was palpable. It had been a long time since Zeb had nestled up with Boo as an orphan, but these two were also old friends. And just like us animals never forget those they have loved. Finally, all standing in the safe zone, in the midst of pigs and donkeys and dogs, we were laughing at the antics of Boo and Zeb. Periodically Boo would slow down because Zeb, in a crazy flourish, had thrown himself on the ground, and the immediate heat was off, but never for long. Zeb would come racing up behind him again. Round and round they ran until they were finally exhausted and Boo knew Zeb was calm enough to say hello without all his crazy emu shenanigans.

Despite the initial chaos, it was a wonderful experience, and I returned home, elated to have seen Zeb and awed by the actions of Boo, who had diffused a super excitable situation with his old friend.

Boo would forever be our white knight and our hero.

Three

My Love Hopi

O h, a beautiful little dog has joined us today. She is so pretty and sweet and looks like she has come from the faeries. Her pointy ears are tufts of hair, and she is speckled and dabbled with so many colours, and her coat is woolly and wild.

Her name is Hopi, and she comes with a beautiful tale about trusting in our paths.

Many years ago, I was uttering a powerful mantra when I met Hopi. I had just walked from my healing group into town. The weekly gathering I attended with other like-minded people in my healing circle had been wonderful and I left feeling so inspired.

As I slowly walked into town, stopping to smell every gardenia or jasmine bloom along the way, I passed one of my local thrift shops. It had been closed the day before when I had visited, and I was delighted to see it was open. It was one of the best in town, and I always discovered a treasure, but I certainly did not anticipate what I would leave with that day.

With every step I took I was boldly proclaiming, *God guides my every step, God guides my every step, God guides my every step*. Into the open door of the thrift shop I went, affirming my infinite and divine connection with the source of all life. I was a woman in her power, but I was about to get the surprise of my life.

Lying on the cold wire of an empty supermarket trolley was a tiny and forlorn puppy who was barely conscious. I instinctively picked it up and began to comfort it. I couldn't understand why it had not even been given something warm to sleep on. After all, it was a thrift shop. Surely the shop assistant could have found an old jumper from the rag pile? I politely asked her why the puppy was there and when it had last been fed. I also asked her if she could find a spare jumper so we could at least prevent it from getting any colder.

This lifeless little pup looked barely weeks old, much too young to be separated from its mother. The shop assistant responded to my requests aggressively. She was a sour-looking woman and told me to put the dog down, that she was tired of people picking it up and that the RSPCA was coming. Unwilling to leave this pup in uncaring hands, I continued to question her despite her hostile attitude. Apparently, she had rung the RSPCA that morning and told them it was at the shop. It had been found in a cardboard box on the shop steps when they had opened that morning. They were now about to close, and in the seven hours they'd had this pup, no one had even given this poor baby a blanket or a feed. I was shocked!

I looked at this woman and said, 'If you are unwilling to provide for this puppy's needs, then I will. Without urgent help, this puppy is going to die,' and without any hesitation, I walked out of the shop with the little limp pup. She shouted after me that she was calling the police.

I had no idea if I was committing a crime. *Could I be arrested?* I could only laugh when I imagined the news headlines- **Woman steals lifeless puppy from a thrift store because no one was caring for it**. I quickly moved away and found a quiet park to sit in. The puppy felt so limp and cold that I knew before I even considered feeding her, I had to warm her up.

I sat with this teensy little pup cupped in my hands as I held her in the warmth of the sun in front of my face, and I gave her so much love. I so wanted this little love to survive. After a few moments, I felt this tiny little rough lick on my chin. This little pup felt so grateful. One little lick was the most she could muster, but she gave that little lick everything she had.

Now, I have to confess that after walking so boldly out of the shop with this pup and failing to honour the sacred mantra I had been proclaiming when I first picked her up, I began to panic slightly.

What was I going to do with this dog? I lived in a tent at a caravan site. I was planning to travel to New Zealand in a month or two. Having a dog right now just wasn't a good idea. *I should take her to the RSPCA myself or perhaps find her a good home.* She gave me another lick and looked at me with her huge, adorable eyes.

I will go and get her some milk. We will begin there, I thought to myself. *I know I can't keep her; it's just not practical. I shall have to find her a hom*e. All the while, I was trying to ignore the fact that I was already falling deeply in love with this gorgeous little pup.

I began that day by feeding her milk from a dropper. She was so weak she didn't even have the strength to suckle. I called in at the vets and bought some puppy formula, trusting as I did that more money would come for my food. I'd spent my last penny on milk and a bottle, but I didn't regret it. By the time I arrived home that day to my beachside tent, I had already named her Hopi-*my little love*.

I learnt from Hopi that animals do not need to limit us. Several times, I lost my connection with my heart and divine knowing and saw problems where only love existed. I had moments when I felt overwhelmed with doubt about how I would manage to travel with her. But one truth was crystal clear: I wanted to keep her. I am so glad I eventually trusted the holy currents that led me to her because she was indeed a gift from the heavens.

When I went to purchase my ticket for New Zealand, I bought two. One for Hopi and one for me, and we hitchhiked around New Zealand together!

And everywhere we went, people adored her. Doors didn't close on me because I had a dog; they opened, and if someone did not accept dogs, what they offered wasn't for me.

One owner of a hotel I went to book a room in was adamant they did not allow dogs. 'No, definitely not; absolutely no dogs allowed here!' He had been so emphatic his message had been received loud and clear. I turned away when, unexpectedly, he called me back. One glance out of the window had been enough to change his mind. He'd seen Hopi sitting peacefully under a tree, waiting for me. 'Oh, is that your sweet little dog?' he asked. 'That's her', I replied. 'Well, we can make an exception just this once,' he told me. This man had been adamant only ten seconds beforehand that he did not and never would allow dogs. I have no doubt that was the power of Hopi, but this story gets even better.

While I was settling into my room, there was a knock at my door, and it was the owner. He wanted to let me know that if I needed anyone to babysit Hopi while I went out, he and his wife would be delighted. While I went out exploring the town, doggy-free, Hopi was being pampered by the owners who loved her.

On the only occasion I was refused a room because of a no-dog policy, life sent me help. Once again, I was shown by the Universe that I could trust in my path.

I had arrived in Wellington on a late-night ferry crossing, and the hostel had given me a firm NO when I asked about their dog policy and was not open to any further exchanges. It was almost midnight, and I had nowhere to stay, and for a moment, I felt worried. I didn't know the city; I had only just arrived and had nowhere else to go. As I stood in the street wondering what to do, a couple passed me; they were all dressed up and were evidently returning home after some event. 'You look a bit lost', they said. 'Do you need somewhere to stay?' And that is how I ended up sleeping with my dear Hopi in a magnificent room in a very palatial house with ornately carved ceilings and freshly laundered sheets. I would have been slumming it if I had stayed in that hostel!

Hopi and I stayed with so many different people in New Zealand. We hitchhiked all around the North Island and had so much fun. Complete strangers became best friends; almost everyone we met invited us home to stay, and it wasn't unusual to wake up and be told my breakfast was on the table and that Hopi had already had hers and been for her morning walk.

Having Hopi come into my life was a gift from the heavens that I almost ran from because I didn't think the timing was right. I looked at all the problems and reasons why I shouldn't keep her, and thankfully, I finally let go and allowed my heart and my divine path, which had guided me to her to lead the way.

Four

Punki Love

We loved our hand-reared emu Punki with his flamboyant bushy hair-do. He was a little waif of an emu who hadn't had the best start in life. He'd been found as a chick, alone, drenched from the rain and hypothermic, and it had taken a lot of care and love to coax him back into life. And while he had never grown as robustly as our other emus, he was growing and had made tremendous progress with his health.

Until one morning, we noticed a crook in his neck—a slight kink as if he had slept on the wrong angle. At first, it was only slight, and we didn't think much of it. However, as the days passed, it became more noticeable.

We began to give him daily massages thinking he may have twisted it. He loved this and would lay in the sand, his long neck outstretched, ready and willing to have his massage, but even that didn't work. His neck continued to become more crooked.

No one in our wildlife group had any idea what was happening. People contacted other bird experts, and no one had any advice. Most felt it would sort itself out, only it didn't. Punki's neck was becoming so twisted it was hard for him to reach the ground for feed. We were still massaging him every day and finally began to hand-feed him. If we didn't, he would starve. I knew if we didn't find a solution, he would need to be put down, and that prospect was harrowing. It was like a heavy weight over the entire day, every day. Every time I contemplated losing our much-loved Punki, I ended up in tears. It's so hard to think clearly in these emotional states and so easy to be swayed by the wrong advice of others. Yet, even though I was upset, I still took time out to retreat to nature. I couldn't give Punki the best if I didn't give it to myself.

And while his neck continued to twist, everything else about him was normal. While we had to hold a bowl of food up so he could reach it, he still loved his food. He still loved his massages and was still affectionate and sweet. I was so desperate to find a solution that I began phoning emu experts at zoos.

I rang every emu expert in Australia and every zoo, seeking answers. I spoke with many vets and sent photos, even a video of him struggling to put his head down. They all confirmed my fears - You will need to put him down. There is nothing that can be done, and the consensus was that Punki was suffering from a genetic condition. It would be cruel to keep him alive. I was heartbroken; I adored Punki. I went and had a good cry and then walked to a special place in nature, one I often went to for clarity or balm. I felt there was more to this situation, and I wanted to get really clear because my wise inner voice kept telling me there WAS a solution. But I was also unsure if I was fooling myself because I couldn't bear to think of ending the life of our scruffy little emu with his mop of unruly hair. Yet every time I contemplated my doubts, I could hear a clear, calm voice within saying *TRUST Kye, the answer will come.*

Oh, I wanted to believe this so much, but I also didn't want Punki to suffer - his crooked neck was immobilising him. A solution had to come really soon. And while I sat patiently in my special place in nature awaiting the holy commands of the divine, no words of advice were given. I knew why; I had to let go. I was so knotted up at the prospect of losing Punki that nothing, not even the light, was getting in. I had to do something that helped me unwind and connected me with growth and new beginnings.

I headed to my garden to revel in the dirt and plant some new seeds, and that was what I was doing when I had a life-changing thought.

Google crooked neck in chickens.

That was the big and holy revelation I had been waiting for that tipped the scales of death back towards life.

I raced to my computer and googled crooked necks.

It was a friggin mineral deficiency.

Punki did not have any genetic disability; everything he needed to heal his crooked neck cost $30, and as soon as we started treatment, we noticed a visible change. His neck had more movement. The kink began to loosen, and within two weeks, he could reach the ground again and feed. I was over the moon, ecstatic that I had listened to myself. If I had left Punki's welfare in the hands of the experts, he would be dead. And by no means am I saying that experts have nothing to offer because I have many examples of how their knowledge has aided a situation and saved an animal's life or prevented a horse from going blind.

All I am saying is that they are not always right, and we have to trust ourselves when an expert's advice contradicts a deep knowing we may have within. We must listen to how we are being guided, even if it goes in the opposite direction from those who appear more qualified.

While Punki's problem was caused by a mineral deficiency and easily corrected, I recall other times when an animal's illness or injury appeared dire, and they were almost euthanased. Or they would have been if I'd ignored my inner guidance.

I know now there is a power we can tap into that is often beyond the understanding of many experts and vets. It's an immeasurable and unseen force that can swing the pendulum from death to life, from ailing to thriving, from hopeless to remedy. This potent force is the power of love, and the more we nurture and nourish love in our lives, the easier solutions can come to what may feel like an unsolvable problem.

There are indeed times when an animal is ready to leave its body, and no amount of seeking or praying can turn the tide; that animal is ready and has made its own choice. But there are other times when we could avoid the death of an animal by listening to the wise voice within us that always guides us beyond the borders of limited possibilities into the miraculous- or a $30 tub of minerals, whatever it may be!

Our wild and lovely Punki recovered completely from his somewhat daunting death sentence. And he grew and grew and became big and strong, just like our other emus.

One day, Gill was swimming in the lake. He had a tiny piglet and a young lamb in his arms. The lamb had swum out to join him after being left on the shore. Even though I had been with her, she wanted to be in the water with Gill. We were both surprised to see this tiny lamb swimming but even more surprised by what happened next. Our adorable Punki came cruising down our track from home, stopping periodically to gobble a flower or peck at a bug. Emus are always so focused entirely on each moment. It's as if nothing else exists. But when he put up his head and spotted Gill, he leapt into the air in excitement, ran down to the water, and swam out to join him.

I watched incredulously, awed by the moment, this ever-unfolding gift we share with the animals we care for. There was Gill holding a lamb in one arm, a tiny excitable piggy in the other with an emu bobbing beside him. It was a scene so magically enchanted, so rapturous with love; I felt blessed by our life.

This is love

This is our life

and I love it.

Five

Gentle Georgie

I wondered if George would come and share his magical story today. His is a tale that can be seen as sad and happy, but it offers us a vital gift. It can help us understand that death is only a doorway and never an end. While we may shed some tears, we won't be able to stop ourselves from chortling.

I cried when I met Georgie. I cried because I could not believe people could deny a bird even its most basic needs. Georgie came to us after being abandoned in his cage in a rental home when the tenants moved out. But let me tell you, the cruelty inflicted on this little bird had begun a long time before he was abandoned.

Gentle Georgie, as he became known to us, is fluffing up his feathers as he listens to his tale. There is something important he wants me to share right now. We may have heard it before, but sometimes words and their meanings can be like seasons—they take a while to come around and only do so when the time is right.

We must also remember that often, when we cry for others, it is our own wounds we release.

Even without recognising our own pain here, this is a story of transmutation and one I am sure you have known. We have all overcome grief and struggle, sickness and strife, and most of us have been broken-hearted yet lived to love again.

Only when we are still hurting are we likely to get stuck at points of the story that bring up our grief. Observe this, and if your tears fall, let your own sorrows be washed away with them as I continue to tell you what happened when Georgie came into our lives. That way, you will also soar with Georgie and not remain stuck in old pain.

Georgie arrived in a tiny cage that I was told he was found living in. He was frantic. He was pacing back and forth on his perch and rocking from side to side. This little love was also self-harming himself and had plucked all the feathers from his chest. There was no doubt those who had been his unholy guardians had pushed him to the edge of suffering and extreme anxiety.

With every pace he made, anxiety rippled out into our sanctuary. I was in total unease. I tried everything to calm him, but the stress that came from him was so palpable it was affecting us all.

I wanted only what was best for him, and after two days, I did something I never usually do unless that bird had been with us for enough time to create a bond. I opened up his cage door. I just knew I had to give this bird his life back, and I had to do it immediately. I felt compelled by a force that was far greater than me.

He did none of the things I have come to expect from parrots when their cage door is opened for the first time. He didn't poke his head out first and look around. Or fly to the nearest tree and sit there for a few days. He immediately jumped out of the cage and took off flying. In all my years of helping parrots live happier lives beyond a cage, I had never seen this response; it was usually far more cautious. He was like a loaded spring ready to go. Usually birds caged as long as he was lose their ability to fly- not Georgie.

He is looking down at us proudly as he ruffles up his feathers again. Even though he suffered for decades on our earth, he revels sweetly in the fact that after being caged his entire life, he never lost his ability to soar. I love that too.

Gentle Georgie, who had been denied any joy for most of his life, flew so high into the sky that he looked like he was heading straight for the heavens. I watched him, shading the sun from my eyes with my hand as he became a mere pinprick in the sky.

Yes, I derided myself. What had I done? How could I have been so stupid? I would never get him back now; he would be taken by eagles. I sat down and cried. Then, finally getting over myself, I got up and went for a long walk to see if I could find my little pinprick in the sky.

I walked and walked until the sun went down, calling his name, aching with tiredness and despondency, but only giving up when it got too dark to see. I was sobbing when I got home. Not because Georgie had been taken by an eagle. I'd seen enough of animal antics around death to be aware of the illusion, and dying in the talons of a hungry eagle seemed more dignified and noble than anything gentle Georgie had experienced before. No, I cried because he had left without knowing that people could be kind and good, and he had left without knowing love.

'I just wish he had known love before he died', I sobbed that night to Gill.

The next day, not one to give up on the faintest whiff of hope, I headed out once again to see if I could find Georgie. There was a slim chance he could be alive. After all, I hadn't actually seen a bird of prey take him, and I hadn't found his body.

I was not far from home when I heard his raucous corella screech. I was so relieved and ran so fast to the location of his calls. When I spotted him, he was flying fast through some trees, but this time with a brown hawk close on his tail. Then he disappeared from sight. I ran calling and calling. Frantic.

But there was complete silence.

Oh, these beloved birds can push me to my limits! I was sitting on a damp log on the edge of the lake, feeling overwhelmed with despair when clear as anything I heard a little voice speaking from a giant gum tree and it said: 'Hello Georgie'.

He was alive; he had made it! I was elated! This wee little bird who had been constantly caged and never been given a chance to stretch his wings had done the miraculous and out-flown a hungry hawk, but how could I reach him?

He was perched amongst the foliage, looking very happy, in the branches of a gum tree whose lower trunk was in three feet of water after the recent floods. I was already rugged up in coats and gloves with my woolly hat, and if I wanted to get Georgie, I would have to get wet.

I stripped off my pants and boots and, naked from the waist down, waded out into the icy water. I'm sure the elementals had a good belly laugh that day when they saw me. I know that Georgie did! It's a good job. I have a sense of humour and can laugh at myself- I looked ridiculous!

When I finally reached the tree he was in, I had to climb into its lower branches. There I was, dressed like a woolly mammoth from the waist up, with the rest of me completely naked, shivering and blue with cold. I was crouched on a big branch looking up into the branches above my head and saying the only words that Georgie responded to: 'Hello Georgie'.

It was a scene of much joviality for all the animals, birds, tadpoles, fish and faeries that saw me that day.

Gentle Georgie crept along the branch towards my out-stretched hand. In less than twenty-four hours of living wild, he had reclaimed a huge part of himself. The desperation and manic behaviour had all gone. Instead, there was a cheeky, joyful little bird. While he came close enough for me to tickle him, he was adamant he was not willing to be caught. I tried so many different things to catch him and bring him home, but every time he sensed my intentions, he moved beyond my reach.

Even the silver-barked gum tree I crouched in was whis-pering, *Let go, Kye. Stop trying to control, and enjoy the time you share with him. You have given him back the gift of his life. It's his to choose what to do with now.*

I got it. I knew the route I was trying to coerce him into came from my fears. I spent most of that day sitting in that tree half-naked, trying not to freeze my butt off, and talking to a parrot in the branch above my head. I told him he was so loved. I apologised for how he had been treated. I told him he deserved everything good in life, and I was elated to see him now so free and full of life. At times, he came close enough for me to tickle his chin. At other times, he would sit just beyond my reach.

I cried with him. I laughed with him. We shared a communion in that tree that opened my heart even more.

I loved this little treasure of a bird who had been so broken, who had every reason to weep, and yet he reclaimed those lost parts of himself by returning to his rightful home, nature. Nature is a vital key for us in our own healing journeys, one we often underestimate.

Gill brought us both food that day as we hung out in the tree together—a sandwich for me and some fresh corn and parrot seed for Georgie. I felt reluctant to leave him as the sun went down, but I knew with another wade through the freezing water imminent, I would likely suffer hypothermia if I didn't get home to the warmth soon. Even so, the cold had been worth it!

I rose with the sun the following day, keen to rejoin my little friend. As I raced back to Georgie's tree, my pockets were full of nuts and apples, and all these goodies I hoped would tempt him, but when I called his name, there was only silence. I stood on the lakes edge calling for quite a while before I finally accepted, he was not there.

As I turned to walk home, I noticed a little pile of white feathers lying on the ground. I knew it was the remains of Georgie.

When I later spoke with Gill, gushing with tears, he smiled and said to me, 'Don't you think it's beautiful that what hurt you most when you thought he had died first of all was that he had never known love, and you wanted him to know that people could be good and kind. You did that, Kye. You filled his last days with love.'

I did see that. I knew it was Georgie's time and that it was his choice, not mine.

Georgie not only comes in spirit and visits us, but we have also named the location where we spent our days in the tree together, Georgie's Gully.

Georgie's story is shared in my book, 'Sacred Journey into the Animal Realms'

Six

Tales of Tutti

Tutti was the only survivor in a nest of three chicks. When the tall tree their nest was built in toppled over in the rage of a devastating storm, it was miraculous that a chick so tiny and frail could even survive, but she did, and we hand-reared her.

There are some animals that live life so voluminously they are like a shooting star blazing across the night sky. I recognise these special souls when they come, and the gift of their presence is often tinged with sorrow. As much as we would love to, we can't hang on to them; we can only cherish the moments we share while they are here, and that often does not feel like long enough. I knew Tutti was one of those extraordinary beings, and this brought up all my fears. She brought so much laughter and joy; I couldn't imagine life without her.

At the busiest of times, when we were racing around, disconnected from all the joyfulness and beauty of life, she would pester us. Grabbing hold of us with her beak, she was so persistent we had no choice but to pay her attention and obey, even if it was reluctantly at first. However, it did not take us long to recognise Tutti's gift.

We could be in the grumpiest mood, and Tutti would restore our joy; we could feel burdened with obligations and responsibilities, and Tutti would have us laughing so much when we did return to our jobs, we completed them with much more ease.

There were times when all she wanted was to lie on her back, feet in the air and have a wee snooze, but it had to be in the palm of our hands that she slept! She was so irresistibly adorable that Gill and I would always oblige. It wasn't unusual for either Gill or I to be walking around still trying to do some jobs with a sleeping magpie in one hand. But we often realised that we also needed to relax and would often go and snooze with her.

She loved flying around the neighbourhood, and once she came back so excited, she was almost jumping for joy on Gill's shoulder as she tried to push something into his mouth with her beak. Fortunately, Gill stopped to examine what was being stuffed into his mouth - it was a worm! She loved worms and assumed Gill would too. He didn't like it at all, but like me, he found Tutti's caring so endearing.

Every morning, she would land on our bed just before dawn and wriggle under the covers, where she would sleep for another hour draped around Gill's neck. Everything we did was Tuttified! Even when I was cutting out fabric to sew, Tutti would fly in, grab a piece in her beak, and fly off, knowing full well we were about to have a good old game of chasey.

At night, she would snuggle under the doona with us as we watched movies, and there was one series she utterly adored, but I will tell you about that in a moment.

Over the years, we had hand-reared so many magpies, and we only ever experienced two that did not fully return to the wild, though they both lived freely as wild birds. Tutti's choice to come and go was hers, not ours. It was Tutti who formed bonds with all our dogs; it was Tutti who flew with us on our walks, often riding on our shoulders or the back of Boo, our huge wolfhound cross. All her interactions with us and our other animals happened because she had the freedom to choose whether to return to the wild or live with us, and she chose a blend of both.

I often wondered where she went on the days she was away, how she was managing without a warm doona to snuggle under or her favourite drama to watch on TV. And I loved that moment when she would swoop back through the open door of our kitchen and land in a warble of song on the back of a chair. I often searched the sky for her on her trips away. At first, I worried she would become prey for a hawk, but she had such a dominating personality that I could only imagine her chasing them. Tutti was so self-assured she flew through the sky as if she owned it.

And while tales of Tutti are endearing and funny there is another strand to weave into this story. But before I do, I must go back and pick up a lost stitch so that this tale will make sense. And I will have to introduce you to yet another much-loved member of our family called Chicken Legs.

Chicken Legs was a magpie-like Tutti and was hand-reared by us the year before Tutti came. She got her rather strange name because she loved to sleep on her back, nestled in blankets with just her legs visible and sticking up in the air. They looked just like little chicken legs! Just like Tutti, she lived with passion and force.

One very special memory I have of Chicken Legs that weaves into Tutti's story was of us being nestled under the covers on a cold, wintry day as it rained and rained. While the fire burnt in the hearth and we were all toasty and warm, we spent the day eating good food and watching a season of True Blood, as you do!

Chicken Legs became so excited she even left the comfort of her doona to sit right in front of the TV screen. It soon became evident that she was as much a fan of this series as we were. She also seemed to enjoy some characters more than others and was utterly entranced with the faeries. We hadn't come across such ardent enthusiasm from a bird for a TV series before, but Chicken Legs, just as Tutti did later, pushed the boundaries of our lives to such an extent that even this rather unusual behaviour soon became normal.

Once again, though, I knew Chicken Legs would not be with us long. I wished I didn't know this and desperately wanted to be wrong, but I wasn't. Our precious little love, with all her crazy, adorable antics, was a shooting star blazing across the sky in a brilliant blaze of light-one minute she was there; the next, she was gone.

It is not even important how or when she 'died', as you will understand in a moment. Though I will say we felt her absence, missed her dearly and cried many tears even though I could feel an underlying current that reassured me our Chicken Legs was now soaring vivaciously through the heavens.

The following year, when Tutti came, a tiny fluffball of feathers with a wide gaping beak, hungry for food, hungry for life, gobbling up everything we gave her, I felt we had been given a blessing.

So, one day, in the reign of Tutti, I came indoors to find her sitting on my computer keyboard, watching my computer screen while an episode of True Blood was playing. I had not put it on. To turn it on not only involved opening iTunes, it also meant several more moves on the keyboard to choose the episode, play it, and then make another manoeuvre to play it on full screen. I went to turn it off, thinking it had been a really bizarre coincidence, even though I don't really believe in coincidences, and Tutti went berserk. She was pecking at my hand, attacking me with her beak until I moved away and let her continue watching her episode of True Blood. There was no doubt she was totally and utterly enthralled, just as Chicken Legs had been when she watched it with us.

But Tutti wants me to tell you this isn't only a funny story. She is jumping up and down with excitement because she knows we are going to understand this. Death is just a doorway, and Tutti comes and goes, over and over again, in a different form each time. She can jump in and out of a body whenever she wants to—and she does. Our much loved magpie wanted me to stop hanging on to the sorrow every time she came for a visit in whatever form that may be and enjoy the time we shared more fully. She wanted me to know without doubt that death, as we have been guided to understand it, is not real. For Tutti, death is like changing a party frock for a new one. There is no end to life, ever.

Chicken Legs or Tutti as she became, never died, and she will come back and see us again and again. The tapestry of our lives is woven with those we love, and although we may all present in many different forms, we, at our core, remain the same-infinite and irrepressible beings of love.

This story is shared in my book, 'Sacred Journey into the Animal Realms'

Seven

Pops & the Rotters

We had just turned off the main road from town, finally on the last leg home after an exhausting day of shopping. I breathed a sigh of relief. Only a few kilometres more down a winding, muddy track before we pulled into our drive.

While the sigh of relief to be home was normal, the flock of pink galahs perched in the nearby tree branches were not. There were so many they looked like clusters of pink blossom. As our 4WD passed the tree, one of them took to the air with a loud, happy shriek. It was Pops, one of our rescue parrots, happy we were home. As we bumped down the rough track, we watched as he flew in front of us. Soon, the rest of the flock joined him, and we had a pink cloud of screeching excitement flying above us for the rest of the drive home.

Most people have dogs to greet them, and we had this too, but never before had we had a feathery escort the last few kilometres home. By the time we reached home, we were laughing with disbelief at Pops and his huge gang of mates.

Pop had lived for several decades in a small cage. He could hear all the wild galahs landing in the trees around him. He had ached to fly free and soar away from his tiny little aviary with its bleak view of a concrete yard. Whenever I saw him, I felt his pent-up energy and desperation. Yet despite offering him a home several times, we were refused, but I didn't give up. I kept holding the vision of Pops living with us.

Gradually, Pops became more and more aggressive towards his owner. Every time his jailer entered his aviary to fill his feed bowl, he would fly at her and attack; she reached a stage where she could nolonger even go into his cage. We soon got that hoped-for phone call asking us to take Pops. Her sweet little pet had become a rogue, and she wanted him gone. Yet this bird only responded like she would if confined to one room for weeks, years, or decades!

He went everywhere with Gill on his dirt bike, riding on his shoulders or the handlebars, crouched down, bracing himself against the wind. If Gill left without him, Pops would land flamboyantly on Gills's shoulder mid-route as he bumped down rough, craggy tracks on his bike. Pops had an attitude and could be belligerent and rude if he didn't like you. One day, he spotted Gill from the air, speaking with a man whom Gill neither trusted nor liked. Pops was already peeved that Gill had begun the day's adventure without him. He flew towards them like a bird of prey swooping down towards its target, and if he'd had talons, he would have used them. Instead, he bumped the guy's hat off his head as he flew past and landed on Gills's shoulder, where he began to frog march up and down. There was never any doubt about how Pops felt about someone.

We lived with so many different animals, and Pops wasn't the only one with an attitude.

On one trip back from town, we found a wild cormorant sitting at our gate as if waiting for us to get home, almost impatiently because we had taken so long. It had no visible injuries, but it was thin. We decided to feed it and watch over it for the next few days. A week later, looking strong and healthy, it was released at our jetty, which was a big mistake.

Once released, whenever it saw us coming down to our lake for a swim, it would fly straight towards us and jab us with its sharp beak until we fed it. Sometimes, we would have to run the five minutes home as if our lives were in danger and grab a fish. On the days we didn't have any fish, we would have to catch one before we could swim. This bird became the tyrant of our swimming hole, and it was so hot that we were desperate to swim.

Now, I am not a natural hunter, but there were times we didn't have anything left to feed the cormorant. We looked for the best options and decided to fish for carp. They have inundated our waterways and impacted the natural balance, and they are also easy to catch if you are quiet. Often, many animals would join us on these unexpected fishing trips - our dogs, our hand-reared lamb, Shirley, and Smudge, the pigeon who'd come to us as a chick and flew with us everywhere, determined never to be left out of any fun.

We would creep very slowly through the shallows, one tiny step at a time. All we wanted was one carp so we could pay the toll to swim. We'd be hushing all the animals behind us, and there were times I'd turn around and see Shirley walking as if in slow motion, her front leg poised in the air, the dogs like silent shadows behind her- not even a breath. The carp would be bathing in the shallows around our bare feet, the iridescent colours of their skin sparkling in the harsh summer sunlight. They were so beautiful I didn't want to kill one, but I often face these compromises when caring for wildlife. I could easily purchase fish caught from a depleted, over-fished ocean or catch one myself that had overpopulated the rivers and lakes and wiped out many native species. As I slowly bent my knees to reach down and grab a carp, I was clear about my choice.

Our cormorant lived on our jetty for several weeks. While he was very demanding, the stillness and beauty of those mornings creeping through the water, animals in synchronicity with us, were so deeply meditative that I missed that rotter when he was gone.

But when you care for wildlife, one animal is released, and several more arrive. You don't have time to miss any of these characters for long. No sooner had we moved into an ease that we no longer needed to carry fish down to the jetty when we wanted to swim, then Duck-duck arrived, and off we went on yet another wildlife tangent.

Duck-duck was discovered walking down our driveway towards our home. A tiny wild duckling poddling along on a mission to reach safety-us! He was so small he looked as if he'd only just cracked out of an egg, and it was miraculous he hadn't been gobbled up by a bird of prey. Of course, we cared for him, and as he grew and began to fly, he would fly above us down to the lake and land in the water beside us as we swam. As he got older, he became much more adventurous and began disappearing for the entire day. Every sunset, I would go to the edge of the lake and call his name. He would come flying toward me from a distance and make his way home. He really had the best of both worlds; he could live like a wild duck but knew where we were if he needed us.

At this time, we lived in a converted shed, and the kitchen sink was just beside the doorway. I could be midway through washing dishes, and if I wandered away, Duck-duck would be in the sink, splashing water everywhere, having so much fun as he pooped all over the draining board. Our home was very open to nature, and it was hard to close the kitchen off and stop him from getting in. I kept trying to remember never to leave water in the sink, but with so many animals to care for, sometimes I would get distracted.

Then, one day, Duck-duck disappeared. I went to the jetty at sunset and called him, but he didn't come. The days passed with still no sign of our little mate. I was so keen to see him that I would have filled the kitchen sink just for him. But still, he didn't come. I imagined the worst; something must have happened to take him away.

Then we heard that a wild duck had moved into the nearby caravan park four kilometres away and was having a fantastic time. We drove there immediately. I was so hopeful we would be reunited with our little friend. We arrived at an oasis in the desert. At this time, the country was in drought. Ancient trees along the dry river's edge were dying. As our own lake had dried to a puddle, many of our plants and trees had borne the toll and died, and yet, at this caravan park, everywhere we looked was lush and green. And because they had their own bore and were not dependent on the rivers or lakes for their water supply, sprinklers were on everywhere. It was a lush paradise.

When we found Duck-duck, he was under a sprinkler on lush green grass, looking like he had arrived in heaven. His chest was all plumped up with pride, and he was waddling around as if he owned the place. When we spoke to the caretaker, he told us everyone loved him and looked after him. They would be delighted if he stayed. There was no way I could return our little love to the drought-claimed landscape in which we now lived. Our little ducky was riding waves of passion and joy and had simply gone where he could have the most fun- I couldn't blame him. He'd been happy to see us but made no attempt to follow us as we said goodbye and drove home.

I was deeply relieved to know he was OK and felt peaceful about his choice to remain in his watery haven. The duck poop all over my kitchen sink had been getting me down. Everything had worked out for the best.

But I still missed him, and whenever wild ducks flew over, I would call out to them 'Duck-duck'. They would fly over, often looking down at me as they passed. Then, one day, it was Duck-duck; he was flying high above and heading away from the caravan park and away from us. As I called him, I heard a loud and excited quack, and he literally made a U-turn in the sky and changed his whole course to fly down and see us. He was like an excited puppy, quacking with excitement, doing his crazy little happy waddle around us. I was delighted to see our old friend, but it had been months since I had seen him, and I had forgotten what it was like when he came to stay.

My stainless steel sink and draining board had sparkled since our quacky little mate had left, and the surface was always pristine clean. I had reclaimed it from our duck era with a renewed sense of pride, but it didn't take him long to reclaim it. He had arrived at the worst possible time-midway through me washing dishes. As soon as he saw my kitchen sink, he was in it, splashing amongst my unwashed dishes, spraying water all over the place, wings flapping at a million miles an hour in excitement and then there was the poop! *Why had I ever called this little rotter? Why couldn't I just let things be?*

We spent two days debating how to deal with the guest I had invited. *Could we drop him off at the caravan park?* We placed a big bowl of water outside the door to the kitchen, but he didn't want that; only the sink would do. If we drained the sink, he quacked and quacked and quacked until we filled it. There was no peace for us anymore. We washed our own dishes on our hands and knees in the bowl of water we had put out for our unruly house guest.

Oh, I loved Duck-duck, but enough was enough!

Then, on the third day, a miracle happened.

He gave us a final hearty quack and took off, flying high up into the sky, obviously onto his next joyful adventure. We never saw our much-loved but impossible-to-live-with waddly little mate again.

The peace in our home was restored.

Eight

Oberon Fairy King

G ather around the fire, my friends. Today, a huge black goat with magnificent horns has joined us, and his name is Oberon. He knows I am about to share the story of what happened when he was just a young orphaned kid who had lost all his trust in life and was still grieving for his mum.

It is hard to imagine that this huge noble goat who stands so completely in his power could ever feel vulnerable and alone or fearful at the changes happening in his life, but there was a time he did.

He came to us when he was only a few weeks old, old enough to cry and mourn for his mother but a little too old to easily accept us as her replacement. He was one of the many kids left behind to die or cope when their mothers were cruelly rounded up from the wild and sent to the abattoirs.

Gill and I have always done what we can for the inno-cents left behind, and as a result, we have hand-reared many goats. Most of the time, they adapt to having a new mum pretty quickly, but dear Oberon grieved, and there was nothing we could do to console him. I spent so much time sitting with him, trying to reassure him, but whatever I did, I could not reach him. It was as if I didn't exist. He was frantic and paced up and down the fence, bleating for his mother. It was heartbreaking to watch him. Every day, I sat holding him on my lap, trying to give him a bottle, which he would always resist. He could see me giving bottles to the other orphans and them happily sucking on their teats, but he still would not join them. I kept trying though. I knew if I could get him to accept a bottle, it would help him through his grief, and it would help him bond with us.

One morning I was sitting in the garden with him on my lap, trying once again to feed him, when he tentatively began to suck from the bottle of milk. It was such a momentous moment. I had been trying to gain his trust for over a week, and finally, we had made this huge step.

I was a little tense at our new-found relationship and didn't want anything to shatter this fragile trust. I was almost too anxious to breathe. Imagine my shock when I noticed a massive venomous brown snake slithering along the ground and coming straight towards us.

I remember doing a quick calculation as I decided what to do. I definitely did not want to interrupt this hard-earned moment as Oberon suckled his bottle. I could feel his entire body starting to relax; all the stress was leaving him, and he was making little sighing noises as he drank. With little hesitation, I chose to continue peacefully giving Oberon his bottle. I had worked hard for this moment of surrender, and I wasn't prepared to lose it in a panic over a snake. There was no reason for this snake to harm me.

As little Oberon suckled contentedly, I calmly watched the snake approach me, slither across my feet and then head away into the bushes.

I had finally gained this little goat's trust and had a powerful lesson about the power of love at the very same time. But, I had also been shown how deeply I am looked after when I stay present in each moment and follow what feels right and true.

I have lived for many years with a deep respect for snakes. While I have never felt afraid of them and always feel a surge of energy when I meet them that feels thrilling and shocking at the same time, I prefer to keep them at a distance. I know how deeply attuned these powerful creatures are to vibrations, though, and sadly, the most common response they receive is fear. While I certainly had a slight apprehension when I saw this snake approach me, I was more relieved and happy this orphan had accepted the bottle—and that overrode any fear.

There is no doubt that our dear friends, the snakes, are magical beings that often come as powerful messengers on our sacred path. They certainly beckon us to stand in our power. When we do, we can appreciate the snakes and honour their visitations.

It is also worth remembering that in a space of love, everything is in harmony, nothing is triggering fear, and everything can coexist peacefully.

It was no mistake that the name chosen for our little black orphan goat was Oberon, King of the Faeries. It is a name he grew into, and that day, after he'd drunk his first bottle, was a turning point in our relationship. He no longer paced the fence or bleated pitifully for his mother. Instead, he frolicked like an excited kid with the other orphans, running sideways doing funny little kicks.

When he was several months old, some visitors arrived. They called in to ask if they could meet our camels; they had never met one and were curious about them. Gill and I happily took them over to our camels and watched all their distorted views about these adorable creatures fall away. They loved them and thought they were adorable. As we all turned around to return to their car, I got the shock of my life. There are some moments you wish you could rewind; this was one. I had no idea how our guests would react and was concerned. I looked over at Gill, who looked just as mortified; he had seen it too! Our loveable Oberon was sitting on the roof of their 4WD like a king. Lounging up there chewing his cud as if he had all the time in the world. There was nothing we could do but face these visitors who surprised us- when they saw our little black goat sitting on their roof, they laughed hysterically. They even wanted a photo. What a relief!

In many ways, their response had been akin to mine over the snake when I had responded with peace and not fear. Our goat could have scratched their car paintwork, and for many, that would have led to rage. I'd had no idea how they would react, and it was such a joyful relief when they laughed.

We certainly had our ups and downs caring for all these animals. When you care for any baby animal, you connect with a lineage of ancestors. The healing of the child is also the healing of the mother, and the healing of all those that lived before them. These sacred bonds though unseen, still exist.

I often went to my special place in nature, which I had named 'Reedy Point.' It was shaded with giant trees, and there was a place where I could easily slip into the water, which I always did. I would sit, still dripping from my swim in the lake and send prayers to all the mothers whose babies I cared for. They were also part of this golden web of life and love, and caring. I would tell them I was sorry they had been taken away and reassure them their babies were safe and I was looking after them. I would share how fast Teddy was growing, how Oberon had finally taken his first bottle, and later, how we had found our little black love sitting on top of a car like a king.

They are doing well, dear friends, wherever you are. Your children are safe with me.

Nine

Emu Dreaming

F or one very frustrating year, our only mode of transport was a tiny Diatzu Rocky ute we called Diddy. While I was deeply grateful we had a vehicle, every single trip to town, I would end up coming home with something on my lap we hadn't been able to fit in the back. There were many times I would be squashed under so much stuff I couldn't move, but on a day when it really mattered, my lap was reasonably free.

We were on the last leg of our trip home, laden with animal feed, our weeks shopping and numerous exciting scores from our local tip shop, when we saw him lying right in the middle of a narrow two lane bridge. An oncoming car narrowly missed this huge emu, who was injured and unable to move. We stood wondering what to do. We were only a short distance from home. *Did we have time to drive home and empty the car so we could fit him in the back?*

We pondered all possibilities; if we left him where he was, he was in danger; if we moved him to safety, he may get up and walk away disoriented and injured, and we may not find him again. We were unsure what to do.

Many people will tell you emus are dangerous, and this is very true; they have hard scaly legs like iron bars and claws that are deadly weapons.

I remembered many years ago hearing a story about someone who stole an emu chick from its nest. I had begun listening to the story, feeling a deep sorrow that people could do this, but that feeling soon turned to smiles. This man got everything he deserved.

As this man returned to his car, holding the emu chick proudly in the air to show his mates what he'd caught, his friends in the car watched the wild emu charging up behind him with horror. They had been waving their hands and yelling at him to turn around in a desperate attempt to warn him, but he hadn't heard. By the time he realised what was occurring, it was too late. The furious emu had knocked him to the ground, and as he lay on his stomach, the emu tore into him with his claws and his beak. In the emu world, it is the males that rear the chicks, and they are savage protectors of their young.

We were always deeply respectful and handled emus with care, but our choices in this situation were limited if we wanted to save this one's life and after running through the repercussions of every possible action, we were left with one choice - me and my lap!

We covered his head with a towel; animals tend to settle down when they can't see. I settled myself into the passenger seat while Gill heaved the emu onto my lap. This experience was a first for me. I had once returned home with a sheep on my lap, but never an emu.

When we got home, I made a grassy bed for him under a tree in the yard beside our home and settled him comfortably with his head supported on a pillow. He drank some water when I offered it but showed no interest in any food. We could see no visible wounds or broken bones and assumed he was just bruised. With some gentle rest and care, he were hopeful he would recover. It was evident he was still in shock, and his responses to us were accepting rather than those expected from a wild emu.

The following day, he had gone downhill and was lying on his side and showed no awareness of our presence. His body and feet were gently tensing as if he was dreaming he was walking. We kept him warm and watched him throughout the day, and it soon became clear this emu was leaving our mortal world.

At one point, I sat beside him and gently laid my hands on him when something extraordinary happened. I began to feel like I was walking beside him through a dreamtime reality. I realised that this bird was in the holy process of leaving its physical body. His spirit had already left and was following currents or songlines that would lead him to his spirit home. The further he walked away from his body, the more his physical shell shut down, and it was happening so peacefully. There was no pain or stress or need to race and try and change the tide. Although in between worlds, this emu was still walking the energetic currents that had guided him on earth, only this time into other dimensions of existence.

I felt such a deep peace and beauty for understanding his process, and it was no surprise the following day when I checked his blanketed body and found he had gone.

All our birds and animals of land, ocean and air follow these energetic currents that circumvent our earth. Many people often describe emus as stupid, something which often grieves me. If only those who make these statements understood how ignorant they are of so much that is unseen. People judge emus for getting stuck on fencelines, pacing up and down, and being unable to move forward, unaware that fences block the natural currents of our earth that guide these otherworldly creatures to food and water. Our earth's energetic grid communicates a language that lets them know where it has rained and which swimming holes have water.

I have always had a great love for these huge feathered creatures and cared for so many at different stages between birth and death -newly hatched chicks, cheeky and curious juveniles, and the elderly or injured on the cusp of leaving their bodies.

One night, we received a call that two emu chicks were alone at a property and needed to be picked up. It was a bitterly cold winter night, and as we drove the twenty kilometres to collect them, I imagined we would be given a box with two tiny chicks inside. It was not like that at all. The two chicks were roaming the garden, and we had to catch them in the dark while praying they didn't escape the yard into the bushland adjacent to this house. They would be lost forever if that happened. Gill and I are a phenomenal team, and we finally caught these two frozen chicks, which I shoved straight inside my coat to warm up. Once we got home, it took several hours to thaw these two out, but they recovered and began to thrive in our care.

While we were caring for our two newborn emu chicks, a carer in our wildlife group was given a third chick that had been found in a different location, only this one was not thriving. None of us held any hope for its survival. It was already very weak, but we took it home and placed it with our two chicks. If it was going to pass over, I wanted it to be with its kin, not sitting in some sterile pet container a long way from its tribe.

I was unsure how the emu chicks would respond to this weak little chick. I have seen chickens treat their own in these situations horrendously. Would these emu chicks do the same? I didn't know, but the feeling had been so strong we had to give it a try.

Every night, my two chicks were put in a pet carrier on a heating pad. I had mastered the art of hanging towels down from the top so they could nestle in its folds and at least get some resemblance to sitting under their huge emu dad. Each night I would sit my two delightful babes in their warm haven, and as they snuggled into the towel, I would stroke them for several minutes until they settled down. As they relaxed we placed the third emu chick in with them and watched apprehensively, prepared and ready to take it out if need be. There was no cause for concern. In fact, what we witnessed moved me so deeply that my enchantment and love for these wild birds grew even more. My two little chicks nestled themselves around this tiny, weak chick. This little waif looked like it was sitting in a nest of feathers. For the next day, they stayed with it, and they always surrounded it with their bodies for warmth so it was always in the middle of their care.

A day later, this little chick passed, but I felt as if I had experienced something so holy. I was glad I had trusted enough to bring this chick home and so grateful he had died in the midst of his own kin. No doubt, the day he had sat nestled and warm, he had been walking his own spirit journey out into the dreaming, and his two little mates had been simply singing him home.

Ten

The Silly's Wee Steps

G ather around my friends. I am about to share a beautiful story that I am sure you will relate to. It's time for us to see what we often fail to honour—all those wee steps we take in life that add up but often go unacknowledged.

Now, let's throw another log on the fire. Even though the sun has risen, its warmth has yet to cloak us.

While some days, we will walk the dragon lines or climb a sacred mountain, on others, we will flit between dimensions from faery realms to the wisdom of the emus or chatter with a wise old crow. Today, our journey is travelled in stories shared around an open fire, so if you notice the flames are dwindling, be the first to throw a log on, not the last.

And as our fire burns brightly, let us hear a story from two sweet and happy little dogs that have just joined our circle.

Their names are Meerzi and Rosy, and like many other breeding dogs, they did their time on a puppy farm. The fact that they ever escaped was miraculous. They were five years old when Gill and I rescued them and, until that moment, had lived their entire lives in a filthy cage that their owner had never cleaned out. The floor of their cage was six inches deep in poo that was so old it was parched white like old bones.

They were covered in ticks and sores and had never known love. I couldn't wait to show them a better life, to bathe them, love them, and hold them close. It simply didn't occur to me that all the joys we were so keen to offer them would terrify them and that the place they would feel safest was not snuggled up by the fire with us or being pampered on our laps, but back in a cage.

We had no choice but to drag a big pet container into our home and make it all cosy inside and after they had been bathed and de-ticked, that's where these dogs lived until they felt safe. They weren't there all the time. We would bring them out for cuddles, but as soon as we saw them getting panicky, we put them back in.

As each day passed, the time they were out became longer. It was slow progress, helping them feel safe out-side their cage, but after several months, we could move to the stage of leaving the door of their home open. They had their refuge if they needed it. Gradually, they began to join in.

Taking them outside was another huge challenge. Outside terrified them, and once, we almost lost them when they freaked out at something and became so hysterical they squeezed through a tiny hole in our fence we didn't know was there and ran and ran and ran. What was so frightening was that even though, by this time, they knew us and had formed a bond, they were in such a panic that our soothing voices didn't get through.

The day was so sizzling hot that even the lizards were panting in the shade, and these two tiny little dogs that Gill and I had only just rescued ran out into the desert. In the big open space of the desert, there were so many small stunted bushes which they could hide under. After calling and calling, we realised they must have gone further afield. As I set off walking to find them I felt sick with worry.

All of a sudden, I noticed an old crow in a nearby tree, madly flapping her emerald black wings as she called loudly to me. She was determined to get my attention, and when she did, she pointed with her beak in a northerly direction. I was in no doubt she was guiding me, and I thanked her and hurriedly took off in the direction she had pointed.

As I walked, I became aware that all the stress and anxiety over these two dogs had gone. I felt a little guilty. Was I being cold-hearted and uncaring? I even stopped to admire a beautiful lizard sitting in the shade on a leaf.

I almost forgot I was on a mission to find our lost dogs when the voice of fear raised its ugly little head and began to remind me what a terrible situation this was, and if I didn't hurry, these dogs would surely die.

I started walking again, looking around me anxiously while a calmer voice within reassured me and reminded me to let go. Miracles and magic happen when you do, it said. I took a deep breath, and as I did, I began to feel myself relax again.

On my left stood a wallaby and it was standing on a little hill, upright on its back legs, looking directly at me. 'Ok' I asked it, 'Where do I go next?' and it turned and pointed in the direction I should go. I was beginning to laugh as I walked. Who would believe the animals would guide me like this? And then the voice of fear said: But what if they are not, and you don't find your dogs?

Could I be going mad? Most would think so if I told them that I not only listen to animals, I also do what they suggest!

I couldn't help noticing that I felt weakened and uncertain every time I let the doubts and the fears in. That warned me that it was not the voice of truth. When the fears came up again, I sent them love, and then I let them go. I did not feed them by giving them any negative energy. As soon as I did this, all my anxiety went. I felt so alive and so in touch with not only the animals that were guiding me but also my own intuitive abilities. I was on the right track, and of that, I had no doubt.

I had been walking for a while alongside a stretch of water when I saw a heron take off, flying across the water and landing on the other side. I thought to myself as I watched its graceful flight; there is no way I'm crossing that water—that bird is not a messenger for me! I looked around to see if I could find my next guide. In the bushes nearby was a huge old grey kangaroo that stood six feet tall, at least, and once again, he was looking directly at me. When he saw he had my attention, he took off, bounding through the bush in his slow and loping way, and I followed him. I was aware once again of the beauty of the day, despite the heat, and of walking and feeling so connected to the earth.

I hadn't gone far when I noticed our two little dogs running through the bushes. They were terrified. But with the help of Gill, who serendipitously turned up at the perfect moment and ran at the speed of light, we were able to catch our little loves. As we walked home, carrying our two dogs who, once over their terror, had been delighted to see us, I felt full of joy.

When I'd set off, I'd had every reason to be anxious, yet the animals had reassured me and reminded me constantly that the present moment is a place of power. When we are in the now, we can hear our guidance clearly; from this magical space, we can be sure that every challenge has a solution.

In a desert terrain, covered in small stunted bushes of saltbush, where two tiny dogs could easily hide, or even if they were running not be seen, it was a miracle I found them. Our little dogs would have been lost forever if it hadn't been for the animals. Crow and the kangaroos had led me on a journey of almost two kilometres right to the Sillys! And I wouldn't have found them if I hadn't let go of my own judgement and listened to the guidance I received with an open heart.

The animals remind us that it is our judgement of not only ourselves but also life's situations that hold us back. Once again, what we feed will keep occurring. Listen to the voices of fear, and then let them go. If you push them away without acknowledging them, they will return—and they will come with an army.

We took no chances after that. I was so grateful to have them back. Although progress was slow, tiny steps with lots of love and encouragement was all that was needed to help these two embrace a much fuller life. They live life now with such exuberance and joy. It is why we nicknamed them the Silly's.

Every time we go for a walk, they yap excitedly as they splash in the lake or river or roll in the dirt or on a dead animal—which is by far what they prefer! They always have big smiles on their faces, and with all our encouragement to move beyond their comfort zones, we have discovered two very happy and adventurous little souls.

They no longer need chaperones in the big world outside, and we often find them coming home after a swim. We always live on the edge of a lake or a river, so they never have far to go; still, it was an enormous achievement they felt confident going alone.

One day, as I watched them splash and play in the lake, it occurred to me that each achievement these dogs made day by day, might, on its own, seem trivial or insignificant, but put them all together; they were huge.

So many people can give up or not give themselves credit for how well they are doing simply because they either look too far ahead or fail to acknowledge that each wee step in the right direction is one step closer to the goal.

Every ascent of Everest starts with one first step at the base!

The Silly's know how our lives can turn around. For them, a life once lived in a filthy prison cell expanded into a life full of joy and being loved. The same can happen for any of us if we keep taking those wee steps and, as we do, we make sure we are our best cheerleaders!

When our little frightened dogs progressed from being outside a cage for only one minute before becoming terrified, to happily staying outside for five, that was a result worth celebrating. The day we left their cage door open for the first time gave us even more cause to cheer.

It is all the little things we do in life that we often don't give ourselves credit for—they may even pass unnoticed—that are worth celebrating. If we lived in gratitude and appreciation for each little step we took, each tiny breakthrough, just like our two little dogs, we would soon discover we are not only where we hoped we would be, but somewhere even better.

We need to focus on now, especially when we are feeling fearful. Sometimes, we can make our goals so big they never seem achievable and become impossible to manifest.

For example, if your challenge is agoraphobia, perhaps don't begin imagining yourself flying around the world on a globe-trotting holiday. That vision will come later, but for now, visualise yourself going to your local shop and buying your groceries with confidence and ease. If you only make it to your front door the first time you try to achieve this, celebrate the fact you tried!

Our little dogs completely transformed their lives, and it may have taken a thousand little steps. But each step led to even more expansion- more love, more freedom, more space, more fun.

The message from Meerzi and Rosy is clear-celebrate and honour each and every wee step.

Eleven

Wild Lulu

A s the crows cackle and keen in the cusping desert dusk and the shy foxes watch us, coats ablaze in the sun's last light, let me tell you a little about camels and how they came into our lives. People often ask us how we got them, but for me, it was the other way around. I was the fish they caught on their hook. I didn't get them; they got me. My first experience with a camel was terrifying. I was certain I would never ever spend any time with them again. They were horrible creatures.

But then they began to enter my dreams. I would wake up from the deepest sleep feeling they were calling me. Their deep bellows resembled the song of the whales. Every thought I had was of camels. Everywhere I went, I imagined I could hear the word *camel* loud and clear. I would walk past people chatting at the supermarket with their trolleys full of food, and one word would leap out from their conversation: camels. *Had I imagined that?* But it wasn't only two people talking about camels; everyone appeared to be. Everywhere I went, the word 'camels' would jump out from conversations. On a rational level, I knew that everyone was not talking about camels. Still, some enchantment was happening because whenever I imagined I'd heard that word, it had a magnetic pull and was deeply beguiling, like a siren luring me into deeper waters. Whatever the camels were doing to me, it was working and just like the sirens, they lured me into a much deeper awareness.

Then, unexpectedly, we were given a chocolate brown camel calf that was only six months old, named Kunkaa, which means crow in the local Pitjantjatjara language. While I didn't yet have a relationship with camels, I loved crows and because Kunkaa was so adorable I was willing and eager to dive into the dromedary world.

Kunkaa was just the start of my passion for these animals. If I had known how irrevocably my life would change or how I would lose every comfort zone to keep our camels in my life, I might have been less welcoming of Kunkka. I may have even padlocked the gate. But that was then, not now.

There is no going back, and truth be told, I would never choose to. Camels have been my wisest teachers. They have taught me about boundaries, stretched me beyond the bounds of trust and forced me to face and outgrow every limitation. My life is infinitely woven with these majestic beasts who are so earthed they are like mountains.

After Kunkaa, many other camels came. I had fallen in love, and my arms were wide open. We had never realised how many camels in the central desert of Australia needed help. Some of these beautiful creatures had been abused, many were orphans, and others were the rejects of the commercial camel industry, either too skeletal for dog meat or too traumatised from being caught in the wild.

Each week, when we drove to Alice Springs for our shopping, we would call into the yards to see the wild camels caught from the desert. I always felt sad for them, but I couldn't resist the lure of seeing so many camels together. With their majestic energy, these animals, to me, were the heartbeat of the desert. There was an ancient and wise energy about them that was deeply compelling.

On one visit, the yards were full of hundreds of camels. They were all huge, but right in the middle of the herd was one that was tiny. While she was a dromedary camel with only one hump, she must have some Bactrian bloodlines—the only thing missing was a second hump. She had long, shaggy black and tan hair, huge dark eyes, and thick black eyelashes. She was beautiful, and we knew we had to buy her. When we spoke to the man in charge, he knew exactly which camel we meant; she certainly stood out from the herd.

When we were able to get closer to her, we noticed her teats were full. Did she have a calf, or was she pregnant? The boss, a well-known camel expert, told us that she probably had an older calf and had been separated from it; she definitely wasn't pregnant. It didn't look like that to me. Her teats were dripping and full, and she looked very close to giving birth, but I didn't know much about camels then. Maybe that's how a camel's udder looks when feeding a more mature calf. He should know; he was the camel expert!

We had a very good search of the yards to see if there was any sign of our new girl's grown baby, but there was none.

We called her Lulu; she was calm and stoic despite never being handled. This girl had come from the wild; her only interactions with people had been with those who had separated her from her herd and stolen her wild, free life in the vast red desert. She had nothing to thank people for, and we did not get a chance to build any trust with her.

As soon as we arrived home with her from the yards, we sensed her anxiety and need for a place to give birth. Her teats had become even more swollen. That camel expert had been very wrong! We separated her into a smaller yard, away from the other camels and made it really private.

Two days after her arrival, on a day that was so windy all the leaves were falling from the trees, Lulu gave birth to the cutest little calf, whom we called Windy.

Lulu's was our first camel birth, and I was so excited, but we had to keep our distance. I didn't want her to get any more stressed; she had gone through so much turmoil, and now she had birthed a baby amid strangers. We kept an eye on mother and baby from a distance and after several hours of checking her regularly, began to feel concerned. Windy had yet to have a feed. Even though he was getting up, wobbling over to his mother, and attempting to feed, they were not connecting. It was vital Windy got the colostrum produced in the first twenty-four hours of a mother's milk. We knew we had to do something if we wanted this babe to live.

Our only choice was to milk Lulu, but she was wild! The prospect of going in and reaching down to her udders to milk her was daunting. Camels can kick out in every direction; we hadn't even given her a friendly scratch on her muzzle, and she would likely trample me. I was troubled, but I could see no other option. I was the only one who knew how to milk an animal, so I knew it had to be me.

Even though I was nervous, I began as I always do with any animal-with a chat. I sat on the railings of the yard and gently spoke to Lulu, letting her know that I wanted to help her, but to do so, I would need to milk her.

She looked at me with her big, dark, intelligent eyes, and I felt she understood, not necessarily the language I spoke but the energy of my words.

Despite this, I confess I was still nervous when I entered her yard. I couldn't believe I was about to even attempt to milk a wild camel; life was constantly pushing me out of my comfort zone. I was new to handling camels and still found them rather daunting. But I took a deep breath, whispered to myself to TRUST, and gently approached Lulu. Her little, well-licked calf was sitting beside her in the straw.

I have heard horror stories about camels, yet this new mother with her day-old calf let me gently approach her, kneel down by her full udders and milk enough for her baby. It was a profoundly moving experience to have this proud and wild mamma stand humbly and allow me to help her. I knew she could sense we came only to help, and she yielded, even though her sorrow was palpable. As I milked her swollen udders, she looked straight ahead as her tears rolled down her face. It was heartbreaking to witness her pain. For two days, I regularly milked her and then bottle-fed her baby. She always stood quietly for me, looking straight ahead, but she wept each and every time.

On the third morning, I arrived at her yard ready to milk her, and she wouldn't let me in. When I tried to enter, she stamped on the ground with her foot and snorted.

She was a wild camel once again, and when I saw her calf Windy run over and suckle from his mum, I knew why.

Twelve

Rani Returns

This is a tale that began its first colourful stitch many, many moons ago when I offered to hand-rear three tiny abandoned puppies. They were only a week old when they were heard crying from within a knotted plastic bag, thrown into an industrial bin on a remote stretch of road. It's miraculous that they were even found.

I already had two dogs at this time, but knew I would end up keeping one of these pups and I chose a pretty black and tan female with long scruffy hair that I called Attiki.

I had been caring for these babes for several weeks when one of them visited me in my dreams. I'd had several different unmemorable dreams during the night, and while my visitor had never been the focus, she had never left my side. Her name was Rani and she was the only short-haired dog in the litter.

The following day I was swimming in the ocean. The pups were in the shade, tucked up sleeping in their basket next to my towel and clothes. They needed such regular feeding I had to take them everywhere, just to keep up with their bottles.

I'd just had a quick splash in the ocean that was starting to get a little turbulent with the onset of the sea breeze, and was about to get out when I noticed Rani swimming towards me. She was barely six inches long and only three weeks old. Undeterred from her mission, with her little face poking out from the waves she swam determinedly towards me.

Message received loud and clear! I plucked my brave little princess from the waves and told her she could stay with me, and that's how the pup I kept was chosen.

I adored Rani, but even that word fails to come close to the bond we shared. For me she was the silvery moon rising up from the Coral Sea, she was the sweet fragrance of the frangipani flowers, and my love for her pulsed in my every breath. We two were one. It was Rani who kept me alive and gave me hope when my life felt battered and bruised.

Even so, she was as wild as the wind and there were aspects of Rani I never ever got close to taming. She lived her own life and was not dependent on me. If she wanted an adventure she took herself. If she was hungry, she caught a mouse, and often on our shared walks she would disappear. I would call and call her, sometimes getting mad with frustration because I had a deadline to meet and I didn't want to leave her.

I remember one day I'd become really angry because she had run off on her adventure and had not returned for two hours. I'd had to cancel going out. Later a friend had given me a story to read about the little dogs the American Indians used to keep, who even though they lived with them, just like Rani could never be tamed. As much as she often frustrated me, to imagine living without her was to imagine a life without breath.

I don't let my dogs have puppies now. I would love them to be able to, but there are just too many dogs needing homes that die every day because no one wants them. Now I am aware of this situation I would never willingly add to that burden, but then I wanted Rani to experience being a mum just once before I had her desexed. She had the most beautiful bond with another small male rescue dog of mine and together they made pups.

As Rani came close to giving birth I tried to entice her to have the pups at home, but she stood whining by the closed door continuously, getting more and more stressed, and finally I had no choice but to let her out.

My feral princess birthed her pups in the hollowed out roots of a dead tree and for four weeks would let no one come close. She even snarled viciously at me if I tried to get close, something she had never done. We had no idea how many pups she had until they were four weeks old, when she began to relax her mothering, slightly. Instead of only leaving the burrow at night she began to venture out on short missions during the day.

I watched her like a hungry hawk, keen to reach in and see if the pups were okay. As soon as I saw her leave, I ran over reached my arm in and began pulling out pups. There were three of them and while two were perfectly fine, the third was an albino and it was struggling. Its skin was so pink and vulnerable and it was covered in infected insect bites. We decided it was time to take all the pups in and thankfully Rani realised that our intention was only to help her pups and was relaxed with that decision when she came home.

We eventually found homes for the other two pups, but the little albino was so elusive and timid if anyone came to see if they could give her a home she either hid or shook with fear.

She was unlike any other dog I had known, and wouldn't even let us get close. JP, as she became known, hung out totally with her mum and was Rani's shadow. I used to call her our faery dog. She had the lightness of a feather and an elusiveness about her that made me question, sometimes, whether she actually existed. She appeared to live on another dimension entirely, in a much gentler realm of elementals, and much to her shock would periodically find herself back in our physical realm. She was here, but not here, all at the same time.

We soon stopped looking for a home for her, but I often mused about a gentle earth-loving couple I knew who lived in a shack on the edge of a cliff with their small herd of goats. They lived such peaceful lives I'd often wished that they would take JP, but they preferred goats.

One day I had taken the weekend off and was camping in a nearby national park when I received a message that Rani had just died from a tick bite.

Devastation does not come close to the pit of darkness I fell into. Sorrow enveloped me like a fog; grief splattered and ripped me open. I cried late into the night finding no end to my pain. The only consolation I could find was that perhaps now we would finally be able to build a relationship with JP. I had no idea that two days later JP, who had been rushed to the vets at the first sign of a paralysis tick, would succumb and die herself. I lost them both in two days. My grief was so intense it left a wound that didn't heal until something rather extraordinary happened.

Several months later I was at our local food markets and I came across a farmer selling two baby goats. One was only a few days old and the other appeared just slightly older, perhaps a couple of weeks old. I was furious. I demanded to know why they had been separated from their mothers at such a young age, but sadly I was dealing with a cultural difference that thought it was okay to eat baby goats. These bubs were destined to be someone's roast. I had no choice. I paid the $30 each for them, said goodbye to my money for shopping, bought some milk powder with the small bit of cash I had left, and took these thirsty little kids home.

My life was not set up for goats, but nothing would have compelled me to walk on by and not respond to their needs.

One day I was feeding the smallest goat from her bottle and I had a moment of absolute recognition. I knew, without any doubt that the sweet little goat I held in my arms was Rani, and that she had come back to help me with my grief over her death. In the same instant I also knew that the other goat was JP.

The goats were about six weeks old when a dear friend who was staying urged me to again take a much-deserved break and go to the national park for the weekend with a group of friends. My friend loved animals and I knew my babies were in safe hands.

Now I'm not going into details, but let me just say at this time in my life I was trying to negotiate a very dysfunctional relationship that I had not got the self-esteem to leave. Late on the first night of my relaxing break away I ended up driving home on my own. I was extremely upset, crying and shaking. Not only did I have to catch the last ferry of the night across the Daintree River, I then had an hour's drive ahead of me along the perilous ocean road that wove snakelike alongside the ranges with its sheer drops to the rocks and ocean below. I did not like driving it on a good day but in an extreme emotional state and at night, the prospect was a nightmare. Not long into my journey I saw my beloved Rani sitting on the front passenger seat beside me, like she always used too. I was overwhelmed with relief and joy. My little dog gave me the strength and focus to drive safely home, and when I finally turned into my drive, she disappeared.

It was the middle of the night and I was surprised to see lights still on in my home. My friend Kaz came out into the night to meet me and as I got out from my van there was no way I could ever have been prepared for her words.

'Kye, I'm so sorry, but your little baby goat, Chia, died just over an hour ago.' A part of me was reeling. My goat, who I knew was Rani, had died just as Rani joined me on the drive home.

There is no doubt I was totally overwhelmed. I couldn't take it all in and for a while I felt as if I was the victim of a really mean cosmic game.

Of course, Rani, also known as baby goat, spoke with me again in my dreams and she helped me put my experience into a fresh new perspective and see it as the gift it had been. Just like Tutti she wanted me to know that death was an illusion and that she could come and go as she pleased.

Yes, I missed the presence of my cheeky little goat Chia, no doubt about that, but I had a lightness of being that was new to me and, in many ways, I had begun to make peace with the numerous ways we say goodbye to others and experience dying in our own lives. I was learning there was no need to cling to life or even to flee death.

This moment in time does have a lovely ending. Guess where JP, now incarnated as that second little baby goat, went to live? Yes, to the beautiful, kind and gentle couple who lived in the bush shack on the edge of the cliff that I'd always wished she could live with when she'd lived her life as a dog.

It was many years later I was calling my two dogs Rosey and Jippy into the car and unexpectedly I said, 'Rani, JP, in you get'.

You see, lives go on and friends come and go. There is never a need to cling to them because love is precious and beautiful and can only soar in freedom and those we love will return, again and again.

We can be sure of that.

Thirteen

Me & Mum on a Mission

As a kid I loved all animals, but I had an extra special love for horses. I would seek them out anywhere I could find them. And often, the easiest way I could get a free ride was by riding the gypsies horses when they came to town.

I grew up in the UK in the Kentish countryside in a small town on the outskirts of Tunbridge Wells. Most small towns had a local common, and every year, the gypsies would ramble in with their caravans and horses and camp for a few months. I always knew they were in town because they would go to every house selling heather and magical potions, and if you were unkeen to purchase, the threat of a curse.

I was frightened by their dark intensity, but no fear would ever stop me from spending time with horses and doing what I loved. The gypsies always let me ride their horses, though if my mum had known, I am not sure she would have been happy. I had no tack, just a halter, and the horses were always verging on wild. I remember once this old bloke helping me climb on the horse, and as soon as I was on, he gave the horse a mighty whack on its bum, and it took off at a gallop across the common with me clinging on for dear life. It was terrifying and exhilarating all at the same time and, quite frankly, a miracle I never came to harm. But these wild adventures never put me off riding. I was fearless if it meant I could get on a horse.

I had grown up with a mother who rescued animals, and in my mid-teens, we took on three ponies that had come from abuse and neglect. I had finally persuaded my parents to buy me an undernourished and skeletal yearling from an old farmer who had about twenty other ponies in a similar condition. They were all for sale, though it was horrendous that they were being sold in this frail and starved state. They were desperately in need of care. I often went to this ramshackle farm to ride the other healthy ponies, a situation fraught with trying to evade this grungy farmer's lecherous advances. While I was innocent then of his true intentions, I just knew I didn't like being around him, and thankfully, even if he offered the lure of a free horse ride, I always managed to avoid his rambling hands.

The whole farm was a tangle of barbed wire and rubbish. The RSPCA had received many complaints, and yet they never acted to end his abuse of animals.

One day, my friend Carole and I had just returned from riding his horses when we heard barking from a shed.

It sounded really pitiful, and we crept over to have a look. Inside was a greyhound with a broken back leg. I didn't know what to do. I could see it needed help, and I knew if it remained where it was, it definitely would not receive it. I didn't even know if the farmer had put it there so he could shoot it. I had to act, and I ran to the nearest phone box and rang my partner in crime, my mum.

We arranged for Carole and me to carry it to the out-skirts of the farm, and Mum would pick us up. I re-member this beautiful, gentle dog being so heavy, but we were determined to get her to safety, and I felt she knew that. We had already rescued a guinea pig from this same farm who had been covered in sores from filthy bedding and being kept in the dark and it had recovered beautifully.

Once home, this lovely dog got the vet's attention she needed and lived with us for the rest of her life. We called her Lady. Mum always got furious about this farmer, especially as she had made so many complaints, yet nothing had ever been done by any animal welfare organisation.

If we had to buy a horse to help it, thats what we would do. We hired a horse truck and drove to the farm to pick up my newly purchased yet skeletal yearling. I had already spent hours with this pony sitting quietly beside him in a run-down stable, gently gaining his trust. He had been terrified of me. He was completely unhandled and, by the fear in his eyes, had only ever seen the worst of humans. Despite being so thin, he was beautiful, a chestnut with a flaxen mane and tail.

I had made a lot of progress in gaining his trust and hadn't anticipated it would be so hard to load him, but this left plenty of time for a couple of other ponies to decide we were a better future option than the place they were in. One was a little shetland pony with lash marks across his back, the other a timid grey Welsh mountain pony who was also very thin.

My animal warrior mum was adamant they could come too. I did hear her mutter, 'I am going to make that cruel man pay' She was so angry that he mistreated animals and kept getting away with it.

We went for one pony and left with three. The following morning, the farmer rang Mum and asked for his money for the two extra horses.

'But I have already paid you', my mother exclaimed as she stood in the hallway wearing her twinset and pearls. Her appearance was deceptive; Mum was a fiend when it came to animal abuse.

Within the week, Mum had received a summons to court for the money she owed, but she was totally un-daunted. While the farmer gave three different versions of Mum's crime against him, she stuck to her story that she had paid this farmer cash and won. The ponies were all ours.

But unwilling to claim victory with just a court win, she did something that still makes me laugh to this day. There is no doubt I am my mother's daughter.

Once a week, just at dusk, when we could hide under the cover of darkness, Mum would drive Dad's pride and joy, his new gold cortina, down to the woods at the edge of this cruel farmer's fields. She would lay down the seats in the back and line the interior with plastic so that Dad didn't get a hint of what she was doing. He was not an animal lover and didn't even know we had ponies. Mum ferreted all the money for their bills out of her housekeeping. If Dad saw our ponies when we walked them home to shampoo and bathe them, we told him they belonged to someone else. We were only looking after them.

Anyway, once the inside of the car was covered in plastic like a crime scene, Mum and I would sneak across the fields, sometimes during snow or rain, jump a small stream and then creep up to the farmer's hay barn. I have no idea why he had hay, as I had never seen him feed his horses, but he did. We would grab a bale each and then struggle back to the car with it, lugging it across the stream and navigating uneven terrain in the dark until we finally reached the car.

We did this until the car was full. The baling twine would cut into my hands, but I didn't care. Sometimes, I would fall over in the mud, but I was as determined as Mum that this farmer would pay to feed the horses he had starved.

That thought always gave me the strength to dig deeper and make that effort to get those bales back to the car.

Me and Mum, we were animal lovers on a mission!

Fourteen

Murphy Soars

There is so much merriment coming from the stone circle. A flock of galahs has landed on the sacred stones, and their energy is so exuberant that we all begin to smile with joy. Several of these parrots are old friends that Gill and I already know, but not all are from this realm.

One of them is called Murphy. She is a cheeky little parrot who naturally loves to play and have fun, but she didn't always feel that joy. She lived her earthly life without flight, and it is a delight to see that there is nothing holding her back now. She excitedly flaps her wings, lifting into the air as she shows us how beautifully she can fly. She wants me to share her tale because there is wisdom in it for all.

This little parrot, so full of love, came to us after thirty-five years in a cage. There is no doubt her owner loved her and couldn't stand keeping Murphy in a cage, but she didn't know what else to do. There are few happy options for caged birds when you are living in town (although I did meet one gorgeous man who had turned his entire backyard into a giant aviary, and all his birds were loved and happy and had plenty of room to fly).

Generally, releasing a caged bird in the midst of a town, or even with close neighbours, can make them vulnerable to being killed by cats or dogs, or even to being caught and, in many cases, placed back in another cage, this time even smaller, by someone who has no awareness of what it's like to soar free.

It was a huge relief to this owner when Gill and I came along and were willing to give Murphy a home and help her live outside her cage. The owner loved this bird so much that she was willing to let her go so she could have the best life possible. That's real love!

It took about six weeks before we felt Murphy was ready to be let out. We had come to know her and felt sure she had connected with us.

You should have seen her excitement when we opened the door. She was screeching so loudly and didn't know what to explore first. After three long decades, she finally had her freedom.

There were other parrots in the garden, many wild galahs just like Murphy. They began landing beside her. I felt overwhelmed with emotion as I watched her bubbling over with joy, plumping up her feathers, growing bigger with her new-found freedom. Then something happened that broke my heart.

Murphy is jumping up and down now. She wants me to pause from her story and bring awareness. She doesn't want you to get stuck on that phrase, 'broke my heart'.

Her story does not end here. Her experience on this planet was completed in joy, but what will happen if you are unaware is that this sentence may very well trigger your own blocked pain. If that happens, let the tears flow and claim them as your own. Allow Murphy's journey to unfold because this is ultimately a beautiful story of transcendence.

When the other galahs took off flying Murphy flapped her wings excitedly and prepared to take to the sky, but she couldn't fly. Her years in a cage had crippled her, and her wings no longer had any strength.

She sank into the darkest hole. We tried everything to entice her back to life. But for weeks, she sat unreachable, totally shut down, ignoring us. I knew she had to go through her grief, but she was in such a dark place I worried she would never come out the other side. She appeared to have lost her will to live.

We had tried so many different ways to get her attention. Nothing we did got a response. Then Gill came up with a brilliant idea. He gathered her up from the cage she had returned to, placed her on the dash of the car and took her out for a drive. As the car gained speed, she couldn't contain herself. Her wings began to flap, and the faster Gill drove, the faster she flapped. Our little Murphy, giddy with excitement, squawking with joy, was back.

So many caged birds become crippled from their prison and will never be able to fly. I wish I could give them back their flight, but I can't. We can only focus on what we can do and fill their life with joy. They can sit under sprinklers on a hot day, climb up branches and hang out in the trees; they can even find a mate. None of this had enticed dear Murphy, and I wept with relief that we had finally found a way to bring back our dear little mate's joy.

From that day forth, she went everywhere with Gill in the car. She loved it with a passion, and if she wasn't out driving, she was sitting on his shoulders, tucked under his Akubra hat as he went about his day.

But this is the part Murphy is eager for you to know. The day she left her crippled body, I saw something in her I had recognised in some other birds and animals before they passed. It is almost as if the scales are perfectly balanced. There is nothing else for them to give or gain from living on planet Earth. In every case, these animals, and I have seen this with people too, have fully embraced the difficulties they lived with, transcended all limitations and anchored joy. The cycle of their life is complete.

That moment is tangible, palpable. It is nothing that can be put into words. It is not even anything physical, you see. It's a spark, a resonance, and often, it slips by without immediate recognition of what is being communicated.

It's only later when you are berating yourself because you forgot to shut the gate, or pay attention, or notice, or get your pet to the vet sooner, that you remember that fleeting moment and realise that you knew on some level your dear friend was about to pass.

We know that death is just a doorway, but this may come as a shock to those who love to control. An animal's death is not ours to determine. Those moments when we could have acted slip by because they are meant to. Murphy wants you to know this; her intention is to anchor light within the guilt and regret. There was nothing you could have done to stop your animal's physical death because that was their choice. Their lives were in their hands! Not ours. The animals we love are far more powerful than we know.

Murphy was given back her freedom to explore life. When you give an animal back its life, you release it to make its own choices, even its own death.

There is a phenomenal difference between animals that leave the physical realm because they have transcended the mortal experience and completed their life's cycle and those that live and die in abject suffering and de-spair. Those who have never felt love seldom complete a cycle with the transmutation of the physical and the reclamation of joy. These animal's lives often end in fear and trauma, and that is the energy they anchor on death.

We have to look at this barbarity. These tragic life cycles are anchoring so much suffering on our planet that weighs us all down with grief.

But for the moment, let us go back to Murphy, who wants us to fling open more windows and let the fresh air in. She wants us to unburden ourselves of guilt and blame, to farewell our grief, and let go of thinking that if we had responded differently, our beloved animal friend would still be here. It is just not true.

The morning that Murphy passed into spirit, I had seen her thirty minutes before, heading with a focused determination towards the end of our garden, and I'd thought something was odd. It wasn't a huge feeling. I would have responded if it had been. It was merely the flutter of a thought, which soon passed as I was busy feeding animals and doing jobs. The parrots wandered all around our garden so it wasn't that aspect that was strange—it was something about her focus that I'd glimpsed.

I realise now it was her intent because what she was doing needed complete focus and determination to achieve. She had gone down to the very end of the garden and climbed up an amazing art piece of a bathtub that Gill had created from old sheep troughs and railway irons. It was high and not easy for her to climb, but she had done it, and I found her later drowned in its water.

Of course, I was heartbroken. Even though I constantly get shown by the animals the truth about death, the human side of me still sometimes clings. But that's okay, and I'm learning and growing too! We must all be gentle with ourselves.

In my deepest knowing, I knew that Murphy had chosen to leave, and I could only celebrate the life of this beautiful soul who had endured so much and despite having a crippled body, had completed her life living as fully as she could. There were no more limitations for dear old Murphy, only soaring with joy.

Now, let us hear another perspective from my partner, Gill. It's about a little bird that is with Murphy now, another galah with an empowering experience of death to share.

On this particular day, Gill had walked down to the edge of the lake and found flapping feebly in its shallow waters, a saturated and icy cold galah. He tucked it inside his jacket and bought it home, where he dried it with a hair dryer.

It soon picked up, and we were both hopeful it would survive. It was in a warm space, and we had left it sitting on a perch, looking quite happy. When Gill returned only five minutes later, it was lying down and could barely move. He gathered it up and sat down with it.

There was little doubt this bird was dying. It lay lifeless in Gills's hands, and, despite all the warmth it had been given, a chill had crept over it again. He sat holding it close to his chest to give it warmth.

There was a large flock of wild galahs in the garden, and they began calling to this dying galah. All of a sudden, this bird, which had been lying completely motionless, began to flap its wings with gusto.

The strength of this dying bird was phenomenal. He continued to flap his wings with more and more force and more and more excitement while his friends outside kept calling him. It seemed incredible that a bird that had been lying so motionless on the verge of death was able to flap its wings with such strength. This was the first time we had seen this happen.

Gill remembers the exact moment this bird left its body because it took him with it. Gil had a shamanic experience, and for a moment, he was flying through the sky with this newly departed galah as it swooped and dived and screeched with excitement. Flying alongside were the other galahs from this flock that had been in the garden, calling. Gill saw there was no difference between the living and the dead. Even though its body no longer weighed down this parrot, it was still flying, acknowledged by its own flock, which were still in our physical realm!

These birds had never partaken of the illusion called death. For them, death and separation simply did not exist.

We can learn so much from our animal friends, and often, it is a matter of putting aside what we think we know and being open to learning. Even if the truths we have unveiled on this journey jar every nerve, please don't dismiss them straight away. Give them time. Indoctrination is pervasive and begins at a young age in our society. We don't realise that the framework of beliefs we have built around our lives are often based on travesties that keep us locked in fear.

We need to break free from our cages, be they bars or beliefs, and spread our wings and soar-just as Murphy does now in the spirit realm.

Murphy's story and many other beautiful animal experiences, comes from my book, 'Sacred Journey into the Animal Realms'

Fifteen

Holiday Dreaming

I love caring for wildlife and other animals and have always had an innate connection with the animals. While I could not imagine doing anything else, being a carer of animals does have its challenges. It is rare to get a break, and a luxury holiday only happens in our dreams. We don't get public holidays or sick days, and our vocation is unpaid, yet even so, there is nothing else I would rather do.

It's easy for people who run sanctuaries to become over-loaded with all the unwanted and abused and burn out. Sadly, this happens too often. It can be very hard for sensitive, caring people to say NO, especially when an animal's life is at stake. But after several decades of doing this work, we have learnt the wisdom of focusing only on what we CAN do, and we nourish our well-being by soaking up and revelling in all the moments we share with the animals that uplift and inspire us.

Gill and I are like water birds and always live on the edge of water. We have moved several times, and each place had a lake or a river within a few second's walk. Most days, I would go for a swim, and over time, I got to know all the wading birds that nested in the trees. I practised swimming so silently so I did not disturb them when I passed. When I reached each nest, I would float on my back and watch the chicks. I heard their tiny tweets when they first hatched. I witnessed the first time they peeped their head over the edge of their nest. *Oh my goodness, there are three!* I saw their nests get damaged by squalls and prayed my family of spoonbills would survive- they did. However, their nest took a beating but the chicks were big enough to perch on the few remaining twigs. And I watched in excitement the day the oldest one flew from his nest. *You must be so proud*, I said to their mum, who was perched nearby, *I am!*

My magical swims may not have offered the luxury of a tropical holiday- fresh coconuts and cocktails served by the pool, with massages and mud baths- *oh, how I do dream*, but they were balm for my soul. I would emerge from those waters feeling like I had been on a holy pilgrimage to some enchanted realm that few had ever seen.

And not long after my lovely trinity of spoonbills had flown their broken nest, I went outside to see them circling above our home and they were calling me. Gill was calling out, *Kye, your babes are here!* While I jumped up and down, giddy with excitement that my babes had come to see me!

Another way I restore myself is by going on long walks. I rarely get to do these alone; some animal always comes running after me, or I bump into one I know.

It's not unusual for me to be joined on my nature rambles by a kangaroo, an emu, or my five hand-reared crows, who usually followed me on long walks by flying from tree to tree. I often felt like some wild creature who'd stepped out of the pages of a fairy tale. The landscape on the edge of the lake had an otherworldly beauty and was a truly enchanted realm: trees white as bones, sunlight filtering through their leaves like lace. Giant spiky grasses that guardianed the places I knew were sacred and kept the unworthy out. I'd walk through these timeless places, familiar with all their nooks. I loved the dug-out hollow at the base of a giant shady tree where a big old kangaroo often slept. Sometimes, if it was empty and I was tired, I would curl into a ball and lie in the hollow. The air was fragrant and musky with rotting leaves and the earthy smell of macropods, and I would slumber there until I felt renewed. Then, I would weave along the shoreline, jumping from one fallen branch to the next when the ground was extra boggy, pulling out Mexican poppies, which had begun to take over and always followed by an ever-changing menagerie of animals.

Beyond the Mexican Poppies was an estuary where one lake overflowed into another. On the edge of this sandy paradise were three giant gum trees that often dripped a blood-red sap. Underneath their big, thick branches were piles of peeled bark, curled in barky rolls like ancient scrolls.

Once, Gill and I had made a video under these trees showing people how to smudge themselves. We gathered sap and leaves and crumbled up some dried bark. Gill lit a small fire and began placing green gum leaves over the flames until they started to smoke. As he turned to his bowl for some sap, Bazza -yet another parrot freed from his cage- began hopping over to the fire, tossing all the leaves from Gill's smudge pot into the air. Gill put the leaves back on, Bazza would cheekily take them off. This parrot was an absolute show off and was having so much fun; we were delighted at his unexpected debut in our film.

But then we heard the snortly grunts! It was Tuppy and Sweetheart, two of our pigs, who had finally caught up with us on our adventure. We had left them snuffling in some undergrowth, muddy and wet and thought we would see them at home. They came barging into Gill's smokey circle under the ancient trees and began rubbing themselves very boisterously up and down Gill, one on each side. In the midst of his first video there he was sandwiched between two affectionate and muddy pigs. All his smudge ingredients were scattered- the fire went out. Baz was dancing and prancing up and down Gill's leg. It was a scene of utter loveable madness that summed up our lives. Living with so many animals, we could only ever expect the unexpected, even on our walks.

And while these hilarious encounters with pigs and parrots on my otherworldly rambles may not have met my dream of cruising down the Ganges in a giant basket of a houseboat, they nourished me. I would return inspired and connected, with my feet firmly on the ground, able to meet the demands of our very extensive love for the animals.

Whether it was caring for a nest of baby barn owls who had lost their home, or a wedge-tailed eagle with an injured wing, or a pelican with fishing hooks tangled in its beak, caring for the animals opened so many doors to experiencing species I would never have usually met.

Once, we cared for this beautiful Major Mitchell parrot. She had been found on the ground and was very weak. We kept her for several weeks and fed her up. When her health improved and she was ready to be released, we began to look at potential locations. The only issue was that we didn't see Major Mitchells in our area very often. We stayed in touch with various bird watchers and arranged for them to tell us when they saw a flock of these birds. One morning, they contacted us- there was a flock three kilometres away at a certain weir on the river. We sped down bumpy bush tracks, keen to get there before they left with our soon-to-be-freed parrot in a pet carrier in the back. They had gone! Over the next ten days, we drove miles looking for the elusive Major Mitchel parrots. Sometimes, we would sit under a shady tree on the river's edge and wait. Major Mitchels had been spotted yet again an hour ago. *Surely they couldn't have gone far?*

Weeks passed, and we still had not seen any. We'd made many fruitless trips to wild locations in the search for her species and had no idea what to do next. *HELP, please, Universe!*

Later that day, Gill came tearing in from the bottom of our garden; 'Quick', he yelled, 'Major Mitchells are flying over'. I ran outside. A small flock of eight were flying above. They have such a distinct screech, and our parrot had already heard them and was calling them. I opened the door to her aviary, fingers fumbling in a rush and stood back.

She took off screeching into the blue sky; the flock had circled around when they heard her, and they returned her calls. Off she went, flying high into the bright blue sky, and joined her kin. Our little wild bird was back with its own species. I was crying with joy; her release had been perfect.

Moments like this fuel you for days; they help you over the heartache when an animal you have nursed dies. They soar with you through all the ups and downs of sanctuary life. Magical moments of laughter with pigs and parrots or long rambling walks with kangaroos and dogs may not offer the same respite as a Samoan island where we could slumber on a beach and be pampered all day. However, living and caring for so many animals gives us other gifts that are rare -an intensity of experience that pushes us beyond the bounds of the mundane into the miraculous and wonderful. Simple moments brim with joy when you inhabit the realms of the animals. Crows and emu's become your best friends, while your hugs are from kangaroos and piggies. Their children become your children, tiny joeys and fluff balls of baby birds. Endlessly, always mothering the orphaned like the eternal mother. Our animals guide us beyond the boundaries of species and separation and open me up to an interconnectedness with all life—a web of golden light far beyond the limitations and distortions of our mortal world. When I return a baby apostle bird I have nursed back to health to its mother, I feel our connectedness. When a kangaroo I have hand-reared leaves her young joey with me to care for before bounding off, I know I am a part of something holy- this sensitive, highly tuned creature who communes in thoughts and feelings knows who I am, and she trusts me with her child.

I know we will reach a time when we can have a holiday, when we get to relax with nothing to do beyond enjoying ourselves. And no doubt, when I reach that exotic location and am sipping my coconut cocktail as the sun goes down, there will be one runty little homeless dog looking at me beseechingly, desperate for a feed!

What will I do?

Do we even need to ask that question?

Sixteen

Banjo & his Pong

M any moons ago, as flocks of budgerigars nested in the craggy hollows of old gum trees on the edge of the dry river bed and red-tailed black cockatoos swept across the cerise desert sky in the last rays of light, we lost our goats. I had no idea then that in the very search to find them, we would save the lives of two animals on the brink of being shot.

Often, when a new animal is about to come into our lives, I sense its imminent arrival. I don't know who they are or where they are coming from; I only know they are coming. So, when we followed yet another dead-end lead in the search for our goats, we had no idea that another needy animal was luring us in.

Our only information was that our lost goats had been spotted at a remote aboriginal community, and without hesitation and excited by the prospect of being reunited with them, we set off on a long and bumpy 4WD adventure, driving through endless sand dunes and navigating washed-out tracks to meet the man who had purportedly seen them. *Had they really wandered this far?* I didn't know, but we had searched our immediate area. It was undoubtedly possible, though any hopes I'd held were soon dashed.

I was devastated to finally arrive and hear that all he had heard was a bell, which could have been a bird.

Momentarily, I felt frustrated we had wasted so much time, or so I thought. Just as we were leaving, we noticed a tan and white billy goat tethered to a tree. As I approached this goat to say hello, I was warned emphatically *not* to go *anywhere* near him. He was *really* dangerous and was going to be shot later that night. I felt a rush of energy and knew this wild-looking beast would join us; he was the animal I'd sensed. I felt awed by all the synchronicities that had led us to arrive in time to prevent this beautiful creature's death.

Of course, we offered him a home. His owner looked at us as if we had gone mad. Why on earth would anyone want a dangerous and unpredictable animal? This pertinent question was one I asked myself. I certainly had a massive moment of apprehension and self-doubt when I heard he had an extensive record of grievous bodily harm. He came with a warning that he could seriously hurt kids and kill dogs. 'Never ever *ever, whatever you do*, turn your backs on him and *always* carry a stout stick. *You got that?! IS THAT CLEAR?'*

Were we being ridiculous? We didn't even have anywhere to live. We were travelling in a camel wagon, and now we were offering to take in an aggressive beast. Gill and I both looked at each other questionably. *Had we both gone mad?* As two people who were already living rather crazy lives, I am not sure if we were at all equipped to answer that question. What I did know and couldn't ignore was that I felt this animal was meant to come with us. All we could do was trust in that process, especially as we'd arrived just in time to save his life. Trust, we would, but my goodness, welcoming this huge horned beast certainly brought up my fears. The worried look on people's faces and the way they had grimly shaken their heads hadn't helped at all!

'You don't want him coming after you, attacking you with those horns as you're driving along,' we were warned. So we trussed him up in the back of our land cruiser as if he were King Kong, and even then, I didn't feel safe. His reputation had floored me. I sat sideways in the front of our 4WD, never taking my eyes off him the entire way home. I clutched a stout stick so ferociously in my hand that my knuckles turned white from my grip. It was a bumpy and uncomfortable drive home, sitting contorted in the front seat, never taking my eyes from the monster in the back, who looked happy and excited to be on a new adventure. He was like a big smiling pup.

I felt so relieved when we finally reached our wagon. I was a hodgepodge of emotions - happy and heartbroken, trying to trust, yet quaking a little with fear. We decided to tether our apparently dangerous killer billy goat on the edge of our camp just while we all got used to each other. We obviously didn't want him killing our dogs; we had to maintain some sort of control. He had massive horns and looked so strong. The rumours had certainly built him up to be a violent thug, and yet, as I sat looking at him, I had to admit, he didn't look dangerous, though he did have a bit of a pong. But looks can be deceiving; I began our relationship by interacting with him from a distance.

My lack of trust in what I had innately felt guided to welcome seems ridiculous now. Despite all the warnings we'd received about our new family member, who we named Banjo, he appeared really mellow. He was completely unbothered by the dogs, who I'd been terrified he'd at least try and attack, and he let Gill get really close and stroke him. He loved being stroked and began affectionately and happily rubbing his face against Gill's jeans. He didn't look mean or menacing at all. How had so many people gotten this animal's nature so incredibly wrong?

On the second day, Gill decided to let him off his rope. He followed us around like a loveable, though pungent pup, even following us through the sand dunes with all our dogs when we went to move our camels around. While we were making sure all our camels were happy, he entertained himself by munching on the acacias, and then he trotted along behind us as we made our way home.

Only later did we discover Banjo had *had* to be aggressive to survive. The kids had played games with him and stoned him for a laugh, and the packs of hungry dogs had killed his mate and their little kid. If Banjo hadn't attacked everything that came towards him, they'd have killed him too.

I was so glad we'd trusted our feelings and welcomed him, even if it had been in a lot of fear. From the moment he arrived, he just fitted in. He looked so content, even when we had him on the rope. I almost heard him breathing a huge sigh of relief and muttering to himself, *finally home*. As I had been guided to him, had he also known we were coming? Had he even been the one to guide us to him? I didn't know, but it wouldn't have surprised me.

Our animals were continually helping me to expand my awareness. There was a time in my life when I wouldn't have even gone near a stinky billy goat, let alone lived with one. It was slowly dawning on me that all the aspects we judge in each other and ourselves, create boundaries to the miraculous. And, of course, Banjos pong did not go unnoticed. There were times we would mutter, *Pooh, a right old whiff today,* but that never became our focus. There was so much more to this phenomenal being, and if his odour had put us off, we'd have shut the gate to experiencing a magical realm far beyond the mortal and mundane.

The doorways to these magical realms are always heavily guarded and often by the wise amongst the animals. They watch us to see how we treat their kin. Can we recognise the holy despite the stink? The holy heart of the sacred realms open to those who can, and understandably, few pass this pungent test and for good reason.

There was no doubt this noble beast, our little love, had some pretty anti-social habits, like peeing all over his face and some days he had a right old pong, but he had an energy that was so wise and a presence about him that you could *only* respect. I could imagine all the trees bowing to him and the winds gathering blossoms to garland his beard. Even the sun would part the clouds and shine on a cold day *just* for him. He was a force of nature, rather like Pan, and I felt immense gratitude that *our* lives had been blessed by him.

I knew I had to trust how everything on this trip was panning out. It had been devastating for me not to find the goats, but to have saved the life of such a phenomenal being as a result of them being lost was deeply comforting to me.

As we travelled with all our animals in our wagon pulled by camels, we became an intriguing spectacle for tourists, and Banjo only added to that. Many tourist buses regularly stopped to show their passengers our travelling entourage with all our rescued animals. On one of these visits, I was tired and had no energy to chat, so Gill went to talk with them. I was happy to wave hello from my chair beside our campfire but completely lacking in ardour to answer the same questions again. Gill had odd moments of seeking hermitage, but he generally loved chatting with people, being the host, and sharing our wild tales of bull camels or the time I'd been kicked in the face or almost run over by an out-of-control wagon twice! People would look over at me with incredulous, gob-smacked looks on their faces, shaking their heads in astonishment, totally awed that I was even still alive. I was indeed a little miracle!

I sat contentedly watching Gill as he stood in a circle of backpackers who were listening to his every word, enthralled. Periodically, I heard big gusts of laughter. Everyone was relaxed, happy, and enjoying themselves as Banjo walked into the circle. Gill just kept talking. He did not pause for a second to warn them about the odious beast in their midst. I watched, thinking they would smell him. They were bound to get a whiff, but they didn't. Gill kept talking as Banjo went around the circle. Everyone was loving him, stroking and patting him and giving him a rub on his head. I was sure that at any moment, Gill would warn them about our pungently affectionate billy goat. Nup, nothing. He didn't say a word.

The wind must have been blowing Banjo's pong away because no one flinched, not even when Banjo began to rub his face and pissy rank beard up and down on people's jeans. I looked over at Gill in astonishment. Was he going to tell them? Not a word from my beloved. I was up and down in my chair; shall I warn them? I didn't feel at all sociable and dithered in indecision long enough for me to realise I was already too late. The damage had been done.

As everyone climbed back onto the bus, I waved goodbye and asked Gill why he hadn't said anything about Banjo. 'Oh, they're on an adventure. It's all good fun; they'll remember this time,' he replied as we watched the bus reversing to get back onto the track. Even over the noise of the engine, we could hear everyone exclaiming inside the bus, 'Pooh, what the fuck's that smell?' Everyone was looking at each other as they searched for the culprit of the pong. 'What a foul stink; what the hell is it?' They began getting up from their seats, checking their shoes to make sure they hadn't stood in dog shit. I stood watching, a little mortified. This was not a smell that would easily wash out. I couldn't believe that my gentle loving bushman who'd sleep all night beside our orphan camels so they didn't miss their mum and who treated me with such tenderness, was now laughing hysterically because everyone on the bus now stank of billy goat. He was laughing so much; he was bent up on the ground holding his belly, and as much as I thought he'd been really mean and that what he'd done was despicable, I couldn't stop myself from laughing, too.

Banjo's story is shared from, 'Love We Live' and 'Tracks of Love', where you can read even more of his wonderful antics.

Seventeen

Juji Joy

Over the decades, Gill and I have helped many caged parrots live much fuller and happier lives outside a cage. It is our passion and a subject we feel strongly about- birds were always meant to fly free- not sit behind bars. In our years of doing this work, we have integrated corellas and galahs who had lived in cages for several decades back into the wild and opened the cage door to many other birds who had lost their ability to fly but could sit in our garden, bathe under the sprinkler or climb from one tree to another using the dead branches we'd strung together so our flightless birds could go from tree to tree.

But there is one very special little parrot who came into our lives who made such an impact, wove himself into our hearts and shifted the course of our lives that is responsible for every parrot life we have helped since. His name was Juji, and he was a rotter!

I love how Gill and I are willing to welcome the aggressive. His owners needed a new home for him because they were starting a family, and Juji was a biter. We agreed to take him, unaware that we would fall head over heels in love with the funniest, most adorable bird we had ever met.

I had never had a parrot before. I had no idea what to expect, and I certainly didn't anticipate the wonderful character that would fill our lives with laughter.

The moment he arrived, he made himself completely at home, even rearranging things to his liking. I had begun by leaving his food in his cage. The door was open. He could go in and out as he pleased, BUT he soon informed us the cage was no longer to his liking. Instead, he moved his abode into an old early settlers' washing machine on our veranda. It was basically a tub, with a plunger inside and a wonky mangle that was on an angle and had seen better days, which he claimed as his perch.

Over the next few days, we saw him lugging various objects into his new abode; in the depth of the tub was a plastic flowerpot, a washing brush, and a hessian bag. He was very busy doing his extensive renovations. When he appeared satisfied with his new abode, he settled himself contentedly on the mangle and preened himself. We were so curious to take a peep inside the tub, some of Jujus home renovations had occurred while we were out. We wanted to be sure he hadn't taken anything we didn't want him to chew, but every time we tried to get close to take a look, he lunged at us. Always, I must say, though, with a cheeky grin on his face.

Often, he would disappear into the depths of the tub, and we would hear him stripping and shedding and moving things about. We did peer in, tentatively prepared to run for our lives, but we still hadn't had a good look. We did not dare to.

Despite the unknown contents in the depths of Juju's hallowed home, we all settled into a happy and harmonious relationship. It was clear Juji was an entertainer, a show-off and loved to be the centre of attention. He would do these funny little pirouettes as he pranced around on his mangle.

One day, I was singing to myself, and Juji joined in. There he was on top of his mangle as if he was on a grand stage, and in perfect harmony, he sang two consecutive notes. La, LAAAAAAA. He had a perfect pitch. After that, we regularly sang songs with him; he was so hilarious. As he sang, his whole body would lift in the air, as he stood on his mangle on his tippy toes. He loved singing with us as much as we did.

But he wasn't just an entertainer; he would also answer our front door. If anyone knocked, Juju would call HELLO. He sounded like a human. Unsuspecting people would make their way around the side of our veranda, thinking they were about to meet whoever lived in the house, but instead, they would find themselves face-to-face with a parrot.

There was never a dull moment with our little love. We still plotted as to how we could look into his tub and carried out these operations on the edge of terror and excitement. It was like being a kid when you dare to do something you know you shouldn't, and it's exciting, but your hands are sweaty with fear in case you get caught. You see, Juji wasn't always in his tub; sometimes, he was in a nearby bush, which was worse. He could lunge for you unexpectedly. You only knew where he was if you looked. Other times, he would be at the bottom of his tub for hours in complete silence. This is when he always lured us in. *Was he OK? What was going on?* We would creep over with the stealth of cat burglars, careful not to make a sound; we didn't even breathe, we didn't dare to. I am sure this rotter of a parrot had set this scene to snare us. He would leap out of his tub like a frightful jack in the box. We would jump in the air in utter panic; the prospect of being bitten by him always gave me cold chills, but these moments were so utterly funny that we would not have swapped them for anything.

We often fed him treats as he perched like a mini dictator on his mangle. We were his obedient serfs paying homage to our lord - an almond, a chunk of corn, or a ripe cherry tomato. He loved tomatoes but only got them occasionally as they are not suitable for parrots in excess. But if we didn't give him one periodically, he would march in during lunch and try to steal one from our plates. He took everything we offered with delight.

But sometimes, even when taking food, he could be a trickster.

Once Gill was giving him a piece of sweet potato and Juji was poised, his beak open, aimed right for the delicious incoming treat, then, instead of taking the food, he lunged for Gills's hand instead. He had a look of merriment on his face, but Gill was mad. With blood running down his hand, he disappeared inside and came back with a cup of water that he threw at Juji.

I didn't think this was a good idea; this was how wars are started, but Gill was beyond my wisdom. I understood, it's a big shock when a parrot bites you; it's almost an electrical fright.

Juji bided his time and waited for the perfect moment to retaliate. Days passed, and it appeared there would be no further ramifications from the sweet potato incident. I was wrong about that!

One morning, Gill was on the veranda, and he bent down to pick something up. Juju flew from his perch like a lightning strike and bit Gill on the bum. I came running out from the house when I heard Gill yelling, 'Get him off me'. Juji was hanging from his beak from Gill's bum. Gill was jumping up and down, flapping his hands around near his backside as he tried to extricate Juji from his arse.

It was the funniest thing I had ever seen. In between laughing hysterically and trying to help, Juji finally let go. But this is what may appear odd; once Gill got past the immediate shock, he laughed, too. Juji pushed us over the edge, but we had never laughed so much since we had him. He was pure gold, and despite his bites, we would not have parted with him for anything. We utterly adored our tyrant of a cocky.

Late one afternoon, we noticed he wasn't in his tub. We quickly examined the contents of his home: a shredded plastic flower pot, bits of wood, a cup, and a rubber glove! And while we were deeply curious to have a good rummage in Juji's rats nest of a home, we were more concerned about the whereabouts of our little love. He wasn't a great flyer. We had seen him crash land several times. The sun was going down; we would soon lose the light. We did not want him outside through the night on his own. We were living on five acres and had neighbours all around us. If we lost him during the night, we may never get him back. We ran outside, anxiously calling his name. He answered us from a tall tree in the far corner of our block. There he was, sitting happily in the top of the tree, but despite having his favourite food or our every enticement to woo him down, he would not budge. There was only one option left: we climbed the tree after him.

That was the joy of Juji; he turned our lives into an adventure and made us believe we were little kids again.

So there we are, Gill and me, high up in the branches of a tree. The golden sun is in its last lingering blink of light, the earth glowing a deep, burnished gold, and we are having a chasey game with a parrot as we dangle from the branches of a tree. Juji was goose-stepping up and down the branch we held on to like a mini dictator as he tried to bite our hands. His little march was so funny we were in hysterics laughing as we tried to move our hands away from him as he got close to them. Sometimes, we were hanging by one arm, sweaty with fear that we could fall, but completely unable to stop laughing. If the neighbours had seen us, they would have thought we were nutters.

Eventually, Juji took off flying home, and we were able to climb down to safety; we found him at the house, staggering around as if he were drunk. I think he hit the veranda while trying to land. He was going around in circles, saying hello cocky, over and over. We wrapped him in a towel and put him back in his tub, and the following morning, he was back to normal, singing along with us like a choir boy.

Juji arrived in our lives at around the same time camels did. And we often went on camping trips in a small wagon Gill had converted from a car trailer. We had a couple of camels that would pull our wagon which was loaded up with all our camping gear. Juji's cage would hang from the side, and off we'd all go for a few days of retreat in nature. Removed from his early settler's washing tub, Juji was happy to make himself a home in our wagon. He loved these trips as much as we did and every night he would sit on the back of a camp chair enjoying our campfire with a baby camel, dogs and any other camel that joined us, as they often did.

When we began to think of selling our home and leaving on a big adventure with all our camels and other animals, there was no question the love of our lives, Juji, would come, but our love had different plans.

As the preparation for this trip began to unfold, we drove out to check on the safety of a route that would lead us out of town. Was it suitable for a camel wagon?

When we returned home, we were greeted by silence when we called *Hello* to our little mate in the tub. There was a shift in the air that was unnerving; something didn't feel right. I felt a wave of panic rush through me before we had even found Juji's body lying on the veranda beside his castle, his tub.

We had no idea why he had died. If he was old, had he eaten something poisonous? We didn't know, but I was overcome with a grief that almost overwhelmed me. For weeks, I slept with one of his feathers under my pillow, and every time I tried to speak of him, my tears would fall. He left the biggest empty hole.

But it was because of our little love, our dastardly rotter, our bird with the voice of an angel, that we help parrots today.

Every parrot that got to live a happier life outside a cage did so because of Juji.

The gift of his love goes on and on and on.

Adapted from 'Love We Live'

Eighteen

Emu Man

Many years ago, I met a man I will remember for-ever. He had the most piercing blue eyes and a long silvery beard and hair. He wore old and frayed clothes that I could see had been roughly darned, but what stood out to me the most was his gentle and calm energy. He was so soothing to be around.

When he arrived in our space, he courteously greeted Gill and me, but then he did something I have never seen anyone do. He went and introduced himself to every animal. As he greeted our dogs, he fell to his knees to be at the same height and bowed his head to theirs. His attitude was so deeply reverential that I was awed by his presence. Most people push our dogs away and never think to honour the fact that they are the visitor in our dogs own home.

He was like a wise old monk who'd come from living far away in the hills, removed from the insanity of earthy interactions. I adored him.

Later that night, as we sat under a vast desert sky around a campfire, he shared the story of what had led him to such a place of profound peace and honour for all life.

He had once been a high-powered businessman flying all around the world, staying in the most expensive and luxurious hotels, and making multi-million dollar deals with the most prestigious companies. He had the best of everything in life: holiday homes, fast luxury cars, and the most expensive clothes. He had been totally motivated by money and power and was relentless in his quest to achieve more, but he had one love that took him into nature: riding his motorbike.

One night, he was riding his expensive trail bike down a small country road when an emu unexpectedly ran in front of him, and they collided. He went flying through the air, and his last memory before waking up in hospital was of staring into the emu's eyes as it died. He had no idea of the significance of this; he only found out later that when you hold the gaze of any sentient being as it leaves this realm, the spirit of that animal enters you.

This man had several serious injuries to recover from that prevented him from returning to his job, but chances are that even if he had been fit enough, he would not have done so anyway. Something inside him had drastically changed. The person who had returned from that bike road was not the person he had been, and the change was noticeably drastic.

He felt an emu spirit guiding him from within into a new, more magical life- one that would see him let go of everything he had once valued.

When his injuries had healed enough, he returned to his luxury home, but it no longer had any appeal. It looked ugly and pretentious, and he was puzzled that he had once viewed it as the epitome of his success.

He moved out of his prestigious home and began camping in his garden. He stopped mowing the lawns and let his garden become a jungle and a haven for wildlife. He started feeding all the wildlife that flocked to his un-manicured patch of paradise. Of course, his wife complained; she thought he must have some brain injury. She had married a high-flying businessman, not some old tramp sleeping on a swag in their unruly and shamefully unkempt garden. Then the neighbours complained. His garden was an utter eyesore. This was a respectable street with high standards, and he was letting the entire neighbourhood down, they had no choice but to complain to the council. What respectable person would camp in their own garden and live like a tramp?

In his newfound serenity, he had no time for the superficial and paid no heed to the nagging of his wife or the neighbours. He stopped shaving, and his beard grew so long he looked like a garden gnome. Once a man of tailored suits, he soon wore out the knees of his best pants, and it didn't occur to him to change them.

He was no longer focused on material things but on his awakening spirit within, which could not be contained within the urban block he had mistakenly thought would fulfil all his dreams. As he lived in his garden, feeding all the birds and getting to know them, revelling in the lush nature he had never noticed before, he realised his accident and his encounter with the emu had honed his life down to only what mattered, and he had never felt happier.

The neighbourhood continued to petition and complain for action to be taken to prevent their once acceptable neighbour from living in the jungle of his garden. His wife left, taking all their cash and their holiday homes, unpaid bills piled up in their letterbox, which he never saw because he had lost all interest in the insane.

One morning, he woke and knew it was time to leave; the emu inside him was luring him out into the desert. He said goodbye to all the birds and the rats and the possums that had become his friends, rolled up his swag and left everything he'd slaved for behind. He had enough money to buy an old 4WD, which became his new home.

He began to wander the deserts, following the currents and flows just like the wild emus do. While he appeared oblivious to the impact he had on people and the extra-ordinary freedom and peace he lived in, I am sure that many he met, just like us, felt uplifted and inspired by him.

Many had viewed this man as insane and thought he'd lost the plot, and yet he is one of the most memorable people I have ever met; he emanated LOVE, and everything lit up in his presence. Even his clear blue eyes were a laser beam of pure LOVE.

We have our values all upside down and inside out. Success is often seen as a big home and a big bank balance, yet these things have nothing to do with anything real and true or abiding. There is nothing wrong with them, but they are false flags many have used to bolster their esteem and build power and prestige when the truest sense of peace resides within.

After years of wasting his life in the senseless and insane, this wise man now lived in the currents and flows of his deep reverence for life and all of nature and was guided by a force that was holy.

He became a tour guide, not a very profitable one, because he had no care for money. If someone couldn't afford his trip, they could come for free; if they couldn't afford the full price, they could make a donation. He took people out into the desert because he wanted them to experience the wonder and awe he felt from living and honouring our sacred earth. His offerings were the purest acts of love. Many tourists went on his wild desert adventures where they camped on swags under the stars and connected with what was real and true-nature and the miracle of life.

He finally had his pot of gold, and it had nothing to do with money or power or possessions. The treasures in his life were redolent in his every breath. Laden in every bare footstep as he connected with nature, soul to soul. They shimmered in the wind and the rain, the light that sparkled in every tiny grain of desert sand and the magnetic pull of the desert emus who guided him everywhere he went.

This man was freedom.

Adapted from a story in,'Tracks of Love'

Nineteen

Andaria to the Rescue

S o many people visit our camels and are surprised they don't spit and kick, and sadly, this expectation is held by the majority of people who come to meet our herd. When you think of the terms used to describe how we have treated camels, ships of the desert, and beasts of burden, perhaps you can begin to get an inkling as to why most people have never seen a happy camel. We often say to people, we spit and kick when you mistreat us, and we do! It is just the same for many animals, and camels, sadly throughout history have endured being worked in ways that crush all joy.

I love awakening people to the truth of camels. Watching their incredulous faces when our camels come up to be cuddled. They never expect to meet a big giant cuddly creature that loves affection who goes into a dreamy space, staring ahead, blissed out when you scratch their head.

When camels first came into our lives, I had no idea how to handle them. I was not a natural cameleer, and I had to work through so many fears even to be able to stand beside them. Their size made me nervous; the strange way they moved their heads and the noises they made were unsettling. As a child, I was into horses; camels were so different.

But I knew one thing: I did not want to put a peg in their noses. Many other cameleers advised us that this was the only way to control these big, strong animals.

Their warnings certainly triggered my fears. *What if they were right?* Gill and I tossed and turned over what to do. We wanted to build trust and mutual respect, to have a relationship where we empowered each other, not work with an animal that only responded because we were pulling on a very sensitive part of their nose, which hurt. Wasn't that slavery? Were we being romantic for believing we could create a friendship? We didn't know, but we finally ditched all the well-meaning advice and decided to try. With that decision, a weight lifted, and I am sure all our camels breathed a sigh of relief- we were finally ready to trust them.

I call our camels my wisest teachers. You see, even a bully can handle a camel with a nose peg; it takes no skill to dominate, but to handle camels without a peg, you have to be someone they respect. Otherwise, they walk all over you. I know this because Gill was a natural cameleer. The camels respected him from day one. They adored him and became gushing little sweet-hearts in his presence, but with me, they played up, they pushed me, they terrified me! While Gill commanded respect, I had yet to embody a healthy self respect for myself. I had no idea about setting boundaries or saying no to people or situations I did not want. It took some hard lessons, but it was our camels that forced me to grow, and as soon as I began to respect myself, our whole relationship transformed.

But in the early days, with little experience of our own, we decided we needed some help. We wanted to buy a trained camel that could help us teach our younger and unhandled camels that we could learn from too. And that is how Andaria, a desert legend came into our lives. We adored our camels and were totally awed, mesmerised and obsessed by them and yet Andaria would show us we had totally underestimated their intelligence and their ability to think and act speedily in situations that could cause harm or endanger life.

On the first event, we were travelling down a narrow bush track. Andaria was pulling our wagon created from a small car trailer. We were going camping for a few days with our tribe of dogs and our camels. Juji, our parrot, was in his cage, which hung from the eaves. He was having great fun grabbing the over-hanging branches on the side of the track. Several young camels walked behind the wagon and they were tethered to a railing.

It was a beautiful Wintry morning in the desert. Clumps of lush Ruby Docks grew in the red sand on the side of the track, which our camels gobbled mouthfuls of as we passed. It was one of their favourite foods.

Suddenly, Andaria stopped walking and would not continue despite us urging her to. We couldn't understand why she had stopped. *Was she OK?* She appeared to be. *Was there something blocking the path?* We had a look around and could find nothing wrong and yet she was adamant she was not moving again. We sat in the wagon for a while, wondering what we could do. Gill tried to lead her, but she would not budge. As I look back I almost cannot believe I was so disconnected from these animals that I failed to sense a dangerous situation. Thank goodness Andaria was deeply in-tune with the needs of our animals. Eventually, we got out of the wagon again and walked around and took another look, and that was when we saw the reason Andaria had flatly refused to take another step. Our young orphan Kushi, who was tethered from the back, had his back leg tangled in a pile of old barbed fence wire and his back leg was outstretched as far as it would go. One more step and that wire would have badly cut his foot.

It was such a lesson in trusting these animals. We would never have experienced this if Andaria had been nose pegged. She would not have had the freedom to decide to stop or refuse to budge until we fixed the problem. You can never experience the integrity of an animal in a relationship of domination because there is no freedom for these wise beings. We untangled Kushi's leg; he was fine, but goodness, we only just avoided harming him, and the only reason he didn't get hurt was because of Andaria.

When Kushi was freed, Andaria happily set off again, munching mouthfuls of Ruby dock and pigweed as she went. What we couldn't understand then was how she knew Kushi's leg was tangled; she could not see him from where she was. It took years for us to understand. Years of letting go of all the blocks that dimmed our lights so that our own awareness became more enhanced. But we know now.

Andaria had a very special relationship with Kushi. He was an adorable little orphan who had been passed from person to person because they won a bet or got tired of him and didn't want him anymore. When he came to us at three months old, he was a little rejected waif - an adorable one. Andaria had taken him under her wing and, as all animals do, communicated with him telepathically. They don't need words to understand us or each other. She may not have even known what the danger was; she just sensed that Kushi needed the wagon to stop.

The next time I witnessed her respond to a situation that could have been extremely dangerous was when two friends left on their own camel adventure. They were in a big wagon they had built and had several camels tethered to the outside of the wagon, but their two young calves were running freely beside their mums. As they all left the safety of the paddock and crossed over the busy airport road in Alice Springs, the two calves panicked and began running away at top speed. They were careering down the middle of the road towards the airport; people were beeping horns and driving fast. I truly felt sick with anxiety. If these calves didn't get killed, someone in a car could. I ran after them as fast as I could, but they were running blindly in a panic and were much too fast for me. As I stood breathless on the edge of the road, wondering what to do, I heard the sound of galloping feet. Andaria was galloping down the inside of the paddock alongside the road. This miracle of a camel soon passed me and kept going until she got ahead of the calves and could call them to her. These terrified, shaken calves ran over to Andaria and followed her alongside the fence as she led them back to their mums.

Most people I know could not respond as fast as Andaria had, and it was only because of this incredible camel that a terrible accident was avoided.

Witnessing this really put me in my place in the pecking order of our camel herd. I was way at the bottom with so much to learn.

But you know what, over the years, I have experienced camels respond to events that could have become a crisis if it hadn't been for their fast thinking many times.

They are extraordinary animals, but most people only ever see them when they are anxious or when their lives have become so tedious from getting up and down every day with tourists on their backs, walking the same track over and over, no one ever really seeing who they truly are yet everyone wanting that holiday picture of them riding a camel.

They are not just tourist attractions or animals to race around a track for our amusement; they are not here to carry anyone's burden, and when you are willing to see this, you will understand why the wise men always had camels.

They are such magnificent animals and deserve to be seen for who they truly are.

Adapted from 'Love We Live'

Twenty

The Miracle of Harry

G ill and I have lived in so many different locations around Australia, and at one time, we lived in a very old stone house with the ghost of an old lady. And while she is not the focus of this story, now I have mentioned her; I had better tell you a wee bit about her.

The night before we were due to move into this house, I had a dream that an old grumpy woman was questioning me. She lived in this cottage and wasn't happy we were moving in. She was jabbing at me with her finger and being really rude, and while she knew I was her inevitable new housemate, she wanted to be sure I didn't have a transformer. I had no idea what a transformer was, but we found out later that the previous tenant, who had lost his way on every drug he could take or grow, had grown some marihuana plants in the front room and used a transformer.

Once we had cleaned all the mould from this plantation room that he'd lined with plastic, the old lady was much happier. The transformer was gone, and her front living room had been restored to its prior grace. We didn't go in it; we left it entirely to her, but we had one electrical clock she did not like. Every time we turned it on, she turned it off. At first, we had no idea it was her switching our only timepiece off, so we kept putting it back on; when we finally realised and left it off, the peace and harmony with our abode was restored. Our resident ghosts was content.

We lived on several acres right on the coast near Albany, WA. It was beautiful. We could walk from home to the pristine ocean and long, deserted sandy beaches. I wanted to live there forever, and we decided to really settle down and buy some chooks. We had been nomadic for several years, and I ached to have a home.

In our pursuit of chooks, we visited a local farmer with a big barn full of poultry, and he told us to pick out the ones we wanted. Much to the farmer's amazement, we chose every bald chicken and every runty-looking little duck we could find. He kept asking us if we were sure, and we replied we were certain - we wanted to give those struggling in that huge flock a home.

I'd had many chickens before, but I connected with one of our new chooks as if she were my soul mate. She was this little bald red chicken, and I called her Harry. I absolutely adored her. Every morning, I would race down the pen to see her, and I always picked her up and gave her a cuddle. She was always just as keen to see me. I didn't understand why I felt this love so intensely or so deeply, but I did, and it was obvious the feeling was mutual.

One morning, when I went down to feed the ducks and chickens and let them out, Harry was lying on the ground, looking so unwell that my heart did the biggest lurch. I was sick with worry. Neither Gill nor I knew what was wrong, but she appeared to have a big lump on her rear end. I was so relieved by the response of the local vet when I rang and told him about Harry. 'The poor love; she must be in pain. Bring her in straight away.'

We drove to his place so fast, and I prayed the whole way. When he examined her, he told us that, in his opinion, she had an abscess on her uterus, and not only was she in pain, but he'd never seen a chicken recover from this before.

'Would you like me to put her to sleep?' he asked.

The grief I felt at the prospect of that was utterly over-whelming, yet I wanted to make a clear decision that would be in the absolute best interest of Harry. Of course, I didn't want her to have any pain. *Should I hand her over and have her put down, or should we take her home and give her a chance?* For a while, I had no idea what to do; I felt so indecisive. It was only when I looked into my dear Harry's eyes that I knew, and the choice for me became crystal clear. I felt all my tension drain away and stood in the most profound knowing. This little love had only ever received the brunt of life. No one had ever valued Harry beyond what she could give: her eggs. She looked so forlorn; she deserved a second chance. She was worthy of a life of love, and we would make sure she had it and provide everything she needed to heal.

The vet was a man with such gentle sensitivity, but maybe he hadn't experienced the power of love and didn't know there was a force we could tap into beyond the mortal range of drugs and surgical procedures. I didn't know; I only knew Harry was coming home.

Harry moved in with us after that. I don't think the old lady would have been pleased to have a chicken living in her house, but maybe she had also begun to feel the love because we didn't feel her presence very much. Perhaps she, too, was fading into the light, releasing all she'd held onto for peace beyond a lone front room in a house that no longer hummed with the voices of those she loved. I hoped so.

Harry became my little sewing buddy, keeping me company as I spent hours sewing up creations that we sold at the markets and to shops around Australia. She would cluck contentedly around my feet or sit on my sewing table, watching me.

Every day since her diagnosis—morning and night—Gill and I sat with Harry and sent her love. We sat on each side of her and gently placed our palms against her. As we did, I could hear life speaking through me, telling me to let go of all doubt and to hold a vision of a healed Harry, so that's what we did.

Within a few days, we noticed a vast difference in her wellbeing. All the swelling had gone down, and our little Harry soon became a radiant beacon of love. She grew new feathers and looked so healthy. She was the best little buddy and followed me everywhere like a dog. I was overjoyed to see her looking so well and grateful for all I'd learnt about healing over the years

I was so glad I had trusted what I felt was right; even when her situation had appeared dire, I had let the force of love guide me, and love is the most potent ingredient in any healing.

Adapted from a story in 'Wild Holy Love'

Twenty-One

Old Booji

O ne day, we got a call from our local dog ranger. She was really worried about an elderly dog in the pound. He was about fifteen, his owner had died, and in the three weeks he had been there, he had lost half of his body weight. He was so stressed she was concerned if they didn't get him out, he would die. He spent every day howling.

I love old dogs, and I was more than happy to help.

He was delivered to us later that day by the ranger's parents, who were coincidentally passing near our home, a hundred kilometres away from town and the pound. As I walked over to greet them and meet our new elderly dog, he jumped out of the car and began cocking his leg and pissing over everything in sight. I had expected a sweet old dog I would help inside who would settle on a nice cosy bed by the fire and perhaps snooze contentedly.

This dog didn't even fit the description of an old dog, though I could tell by the grey in his muzzle that he was elderly, but he was full of life. He looked like a cocky thug of a street dog with a big attitude problem. His deliverers handed me his lead, and I couldn't help but notice an expression of relief that they no longer had to put up with him. They also drove away really fast, and it did occur to me it was in case I gave him back.

I was about to lead him inside when he lunged on his lead with such brute force he got away from me and chased a young rooster, which he sadly killed. I was mortified and devastated, but as I went to grab his lead, he saw our donkey Bella heading our way. He charged over to Bella, snapping at her ankles and barking furiously. She gave him the biggest kick with her back legs, and this old dog flew through the air. I was so worried he was hurt; he could have broken limbs. I didn't blame Bella. I felt like booting him too, but despite this significant knock, he returned ready to have another go at her, and she kicked him again, even harder. By this time, Gill had heard my desperate cries for help and come running. Together, we caught this old dog and put him on a very secure lead.

There was no way we could keep him. We had a sanctuary of animals; we couldn't risk their lives to make sure his life was easier. He wasn't even desexed. He looked like a dog who had lived on the streets; he certainly had never been a pampered pooch. I could imagine him pissing up every lamppost on his street and ready to fight over every bitch. My goodness, he had to go.

It was very hard for me to phone the ranger and tell her we could not keep him. We never usually give up on any animal, but at that moment, I couldn't see any way he could stay. The ranger told us he would be picked up in a few hours. Needing a break from the trauma and chaos this dog had already inflicted on us, I put him in an empty animal yard I knew he couldn't get out of so I could go and make a cup of tea. He went crazy, howling, barking, and running up and down the fence line. He was so distraught that I got him out again and stood with him on a lead, wondering what to do with him.

I'd noticed he had a lot of ticks, so Gill and I decided to give him a warm bath and de-tick him. He had been living in a small pen for the last few weeks and stunk. This old boy loved being pampered and preened, and he even sat down in the warm water. It was good to see him relax. When we'd lifted him into the bath, his body had felt so tense. This boy had been living in tension for a very long time. I also got the feeling he had never had a bath before. After we'd dried him and given him a brush, I was concerned he might get cold, so I put him in a nice fleecy jacket. I still had an hour before the little rotter left my life, and peace was restored at our sanctuary. I decided to take him for a walk, just him and me, no donkeys anywhere, and a long way away from our chickens. We went for a good long walk; I knew he would be going back to his small concrete pen; at least if he'd had some exercise, it may help him settle on his return. He loved his walk and felt calm for the first time since he arrived. As we were getting close to his pick-up time, we headed home. We didn't have long to wait before his ride arrived.

As the car pulled up to collect him, I looked down at him standing peacefully by my side, all snuggly and clean in his fluffy jacket, and he gave me a look that was so beseeching; it communicated his broken heart, his anxiety and his panic at being returned to his concrete cell.

I knew at that moment I could not send him back. I had to give this old boy a chance. If we didn't, no one would. This bruiser of a dog was not some sweet little adorable love that would be quickly adopted, but Gill and I always say, *It's easy to love the loveable*. Well, here was our chance to love the seemingly unloveable.

I looked into his eyes and told him he would have to leave his wild ways behind if he wanted to stay. There would be no more killing, and he would have to listen to us when we asked him to do something. It was up to him if he got to stay, but we would at least give him a chance. I didn't let him lose eye contact. Each time he went to look away, I would gently guide his face back towards me. He needed to know there could be no compromise for us. He had to get this; there was no second chance. We had already experienced one killing too many.

At that moment, I didn't know if he would get it, but the choice to give him a chance felt good. It felt right. I don't think I would have had any inner peace if I had sent him back. His death would have been inevitable and tragic.

For the next six weeks, I kept him on a lead. Oh, it was hard work, but this is what we do to guide difficult animals through their integration into our sanctuary. When I was sewing up clothes for our business, he sat on his bed on a lead. At night, he slept on a bed on a lead. We had endless walks throughout the day, where I would teach him various commands. We also spent time amongst the chickens, where I kept him on a very tight and short lead. Every time he lunged, he got yanked back and told NO. When he passed them without responding, I would give him so much praise. I made the praise the focus.

I think Booji had quickly decided when I gave him that ultimatum that he was where he wanted to live because he learnt so fast. People say you cannot teach an old dog new tricks, which is untrue. For Booji, everything in our sanctuary was new - living in harmony with other animals, all the love, his cosy bed, his place at our hearth, a life lived without stress or anxiety from never knowing what frame of mind his unstable owner would be in. He adapted and transformed, eager to be a part of our loving tribe; he shed his old ways like a snake shed its skin.

And I found out a bit about his past life. He had come from a place that was not far away. His owner had died, and while his wife was still alive, she had been institutionalised.

Booji had survived in a violent and unpredictable environment and often had to fend for himself. He'd never known peace of mind from having stability or certainty. The husband and wife had fought a lot, and their fights were loud and destructive. Those who shared Booji's history agreed that this dog had not had an easy life.

One day, after the wife had been released from hospital, she visited Booji.

She felt erratic and unstable, and her conversation was hard to follow, but she obviously loved Booji. She was happy he was with us, but as soon as he saw her, he made a very wide circle around her and went and hid. Beyond a fleeting glimpse, she didn't get to see him, and he didn't come out until long after she had gone. It wasn't a happy reunion for him, and I reassured him there was no going back. He was part of our tribe now.

This old boy shed his old dysfunctional ways so fast. Within two weeks, he was walking through the chickens and not even noticing them. It was as if they didn't exist.

People also say that once an animal has killed an animal and tasted blood, you can never change them. This statement is also untrue. Since Booji, I have trained numerous dogs who once killed other animals to coexist and live in harmony. I know this can be done. Old Booji was perhaps the first dog we discovered this with - our old killer who found the light.

He was a transformed dog when he finally earned his right to be let off his lead. Of course, we kept a very close eye on him. He had to show us we could totally trust him, and over time, he did. I saw him happily coexisting with our hand-reared joeys and sleeping with some chickens. I even saw a pet pigeon land on his head, and he did not react.

He put all his weight on again, and many of my customers got to know him. When Gill and I did a photo shoot of all my clothing creations, Booji was always beside me as I modelled my dresses. Every photo, there he is, my lovely little rotter. He was so adoring he followed me everywhere, even to the loo.

The scars he'd worn from the battlefield of his life began to fade. And how can you remain a wily street dog when you're wearing a warm, fluffy jacket? How can you stay a hooligan when you're cossetted and loved, snoring and safe beside a warm fire? I loved Booji; he became my constant shadow, always there, always with me, my little, much-loved mate.

The last two years of his life, I know, were his best. He bloomed with us, and while he may have lived for many years as a street dog, he ended his cycle on earth as a deeply loved pampered pooch.

Adapted from a story in 'Sacred Journey into the Animal Realms.'

Twenty-Two

Our Lion King Sax

D ozer is a dog that came into our lives several years ago in a very serendipitous way. It was one of those occasions when I dallied on the edge of my decision to welcome him for quite some time. Every time I thought my mind was made up, something occurred to flip my latest decision on its head.

I knew he had been at the pound for a long time, and despite numerous people sharing his post on social media with so much enthusiasm to find this dog a home, he still didn't have one.

His picture kept turning up unexpectedly in my social media newsfeed, and while I was holding space for him to find his perfect home, I didn't think that would be with me. I kept checking on him to see if he had found his home, but alas, he never had. Then I dreamt about him walking by my side. A few days later, when I couldn't stop thinking about him, I asked Gill how he felt about offering this unwanted dog a home. He was keen, so we agreed to take on Dozer.

We didn't know anything about this dog's background. Although dogs this size are often used for hunting, and we presumed this giant mastiff x wolfhound had most likely killed pigs. The rescue group who had him confirmed he had come from a hunting background, yet was very gentle and sweet. Although they adored him and were keen to find him a great home, they were also aware we had a sanctuary. They didn't want to risk the lives of any of our animals, and neither did we, but the feeling to get him was still so strong.

We had many uncertainties and numerous doubts, but each time we let go of the prospect of having him, he would spring back jubilantly and land like a giant, playful pup in our arms.

I hadn't realised he needed desexing, which was an extra cost we couldn't really afford, but then some beautiful supporters offered to pay. We didn't know how we could get him. We lived a long way from major towns. When I let the rescue group know, they replied they would deliver him to our door! I was astounded at this; they operated their rescue organisation in a town almost one thousand kilometres away. Every obstacle that appeared was resolved, though, of course, we still didn't know much about how he would respond to other animals. All I knew was that getting him felt incredibly right. When everything flows to make something happen, we truly have to let go of our resistance and open our arms in trust, and that's what we finally did.

It took several weeks before he came to us. During that time, I regularly connected with him energetically. I reassured him he would love living with us and let him know we had clear boundaries. We did not accept killing; he needed to leave that energy behind.

There was definitely a familiarity to him when he arrived, even though he was nervous and unsure and wanted to get back into the car that had delivered him. Thresholds can be scary! We understood that, but he soon forgot his fears when we took him swimming in the river. All his bottled-up energy began to flow. He loved the water, and his apprehension about this major change in his life slowly unravelled in all the love.

I had not expected him to be so big. I had seen pictures of him, but they had given me no gauge of his size. His paws were almost as big as my hands, and he made our big dogs look like tiddlers! I remember feeling quite daunted when I saw him. I had never had such a giant dog. Taking him on and welcoming him into our harmonious haven with so many other animals that depended on us was a big responsibility. Of course, we kept him on a lead, but we could see that he had barely any interest, other than curiosity, in any of our animals. He even behaved when he saw our chickens, which was encouraging for us to see.

We felt as if a lion had moved into our midst, and at this time in our lives, lion energy was coming at us from everywhere. A few days before, Gill had found on an early settler's old and long since used rubbish tip a large cast iron lion that looked like a doorstop. We had it proudly displayed in our home. Then, a friend sent us a beautiful card with a lion that I had hung on our wall.

We both sensed that to create harmony with this new dog, we had to be totally aligned with harmony ourselves. Our inner growth is always the key with a challenging animal - they force us to grow. We have to stand in a more empowered presence than their dysfunction, and I knew this dog had come to push us into more personal empowerment. We had recently experienced some challenges that had left us feeling quite forlorn and unsure of our worth. Well, the time of licking our wounds was over; this dog would be our gauge if we got out of balance, and we would see our harmony mirrored in his behaviour.

One morning, not long after he'd arrived, Gill and I had to visit a place we had been clearing some energy. Not wanting to leave our new dog, Dozer, behind, we let him ride in the back of the Ute, which he had made perfectly clear he loved to do.

In fact, in those first few weeks with us, his favourite hangout was the Ute. It was the place he felt safe. There was no rush for him to settle in. It would happen in his time. He would spend an hour with us, and then he would return to the Ute, sleep for an hour or two, and then join us again. It was his way of acclimatising to his new home. We may have been a big welcoming tribe, but it was a long time since Dozer had had a family, if he had ever had one, and he needed that time to adjust.

On this particular day, we set off with Dozer riding in the back. The day flowed, we did what we needed, and everything went well. We were driving home when Gill decided to pull up and check a dead kangaroo on the side of the dirt road to make sure it didn't have a joey in its pouch.

No sooner had Gill pulled up than Dozer began flinging himself around in the back of the Ute at the end of his chain. He managed to get his collar over his head and jump out of our 4WD. He then pounced on the kangaroo and started shaking it around. The strength in his jaws was horrifying, and the only blessing of this incident was that the kangaroo was already dead! His behaviour deeply disturbed me; I could hear the crunch of the bones. Dozer had behaved as if he was possessed.

I felt churned up as we drove home. It had taken force to bring this dog under control, and I felt really anxious that we had taken on too much. It was Gill who reminded me once again that we had to trust. It had felt so right to give him a home and with patience and love, it was inevitable that this unruly force of a dog, would come good.

In a space of love, everything heals!

I wanted to believe that, though it felt as if we'd had a zombie in the back of the vehicle and I was pretty damn glum.

But, once again, as in all things, this experience had very powerful learning. We knew without doubt that Dozer could not be trusted with kangaroos at the present time. But there is a map to follow, reflected in this dog's story. That's why he is standing by my side, wanting me to share it—grizzly bones and all!

I had fallen in love with a noble lion king of a dog, and that's the self he had come to us to reclaim.

The rescue group had contacted me as they'd learned more about his story. He was a failed hunting dog that had been abandoned. As a puppy, pig hunters had shut him in a cage and fired guns around him in a cruel and ludicrous attempt to desensitise him. This brutality gave him PTSD. With every loud noise, he would tremble like a baby and try to scramble for cover. Every lightning strike, I would sit by this big hairy mutt and hold him as he shook.

But I had also learnt of a woman who had given him a home, and while out on a walk in her local park, he had chased a kangaroo and savagely killed it in front of her. Deeply traumatised, she had returned him to the rescue group.

It was evident he could not be trusted, especially with kangaroos, and I knew we would have to progress slowly. Take each day as it came and not look too far ahead. His behaviour would change, but for the moment, every time he sat in the back of the Ute, he was on a chain; he had to earn the liberty of his freedom. When we walked him, it was on a lead. I desperately wanted to work with him. After hearing more of his story, I felt the deepest compassion for the wounded young pup he had been, but I couldn't get the image of him tearing apart that dead kangaroo.

But then a remarkable event occurred, just a day after I almost lost my faith in him, and it verged on the biblical.

I was still feeling down. We were dealing with a dog that was so big and powerful, and it was a huge responsibility. While Gill continued to reassure me that Sax would soon leave his old ways behind, I was keeping an eye on the dogs as they ate their food, checking that none of the fatties were gobbling leftovers. When I went outside to check on Sax, I couldn't believe my eyes. There he was, sitting beside our young orphaned lamb Eve, and they were both peacefully eating out of his bowl. The words came to me instantly: the lion will lie down with the lamb.

At that moment, I knew I was being given a powerful message from Spirit, and I understood the lessons of this dog and why he had come into our lives.

I was also clear he wanted his name to change. In truth, I had struggled with his name. It had a frequency I didn't align with, one I would like him to leave behind. He may have needed to be a Dozer in his past, but he was in a space of kindness and love now where he would be treated with sensitivity.

The following morning, as I was out walking him, I heard, loud and clear, Sax, my name is Sax. It felt so strong, so right, so lion king-ish that I ran back and woke Gill up to tell him. His response was yes, that's it! Sax had finally come home.

Sax is wagging his huge tail beside me, and I feel his excitement. He is happy I have understood.

He came to lead us over the threshold into a new reality. He came to remind us that in every moment, we are offered a choice. Choosing to have Sax in our lives could only happen if we aligned ourselves with the sacred and lived in harmony. There was no more room for procrastination, for wobbling from our path, for being less than we knew we could be. We had to keep our energy clear and flowing because he would reflect us.

I couldn't help thinking about a book I had read many years ago (Initiation by Elizabeth Haich). It was written by a woman who had past life memories of working with the sacred lions in the temples of Egypt. One had to be totally aligned to work with the lions; otherwise, they would kill you. It was as black and white as that. You either had it, or you didn't. There was no room for fear, and it took focus, discipline and dedication to prepare oneself to be in their presence.

We may not have a lion living with us, but we had the next best thing. Sax was here to help us align with our higher selves and lead us all into a new reality—one overflowing with love, and he did!

Adapted from a story in 'Sacred Journey into the Animal Realms.'

Twenty-Three

Billy Beloved our Giant Bull

B illy Beloved is a bull, and despite his enormous size, he is one of the most sensitive animals here. He has always been a guardian of the animals, especially his friends, the sheep. However, he wasn't always so big and strong. In fact, when he was little, he was so frail he almost died. But his story reminds us of the power we have when we hold the highest vision.

He came to us when he was only a couple of days old. A woman found him lying alone on a long, dry stretch of road. The country was in drought, and it was blisteringly hot. His eyes looked glazed and sunken, and his mouth was parched dry. She could see far across the vast, flat desert plains, and no other cows were around. If she didn't take him, he would soon become prey to the eagles and crows who were already waiting.

Serendipitously, our angel of mercy found her way to our haven and left Billy Beloved with us.

For his first two weeks, he thrived. He bounced around our garden, took himself off for wild runs, croaked cutely like a little frog when he got excited and filled our lives with delight.

Then, one morning, he was not his usual happy self. It was such a subtle difference it could have been easily missed. I certainly hoped it was my imagination, but deep down, I knew something was wrong and I felt stressed.

I watched his every breath. *Was he breathing too fast? Did he have a temperature? Had he drunk every drop of milk?* And every day, something more was wrong. He was weaker. He hadn't drunk all his milk. Then, his body began to tremble and shake. There was no doubt he needed physical help. He had a course of antibiotics, and yet nothing appeared to work. Despite doing every-thing I could, I feared we would lose Billy.

I was crying as I stroked him. I didn't want our little love to die, but death looked imminent. He was lying on a blanket, panting heavily, and his temperature was high. There I was, imagining life without him, when suddenly, I heard some words speaking clearly to me from within. *Why do you imagine the worst? Hold the energy for me to heal!*

I felt like I had been doused in icy cold water. It was a wake-up slap. I had been wailing by Billy's deathbed as if he was already long gone. What had I been doing? I had been so tangled up in my emotions that nothing I did was clear. I shifted my focus, and as I did, my body relaxed. I held a vision of me and Billy. I was standing beside him and he was big and healthy and strong.

Ten minutes later, Billy was sitting up! He looked so bright that I gave him a bowl of hay, which he ate. Then my wobbly love got up. I had been on the verge of burying him, but instead, he was exploring the garden!

I had been holding the space for his death and not for his vibrant life. But even if he had completed his life and was about to pass over, I had held such a fragmented energy for him. *Gosh, I had a lot to learn*.

And Billy did grow, so big he looks like a mountain. He has spent the last six years looking after our herd of rescued sheep. They adore him and follow him every-where, and in all the years he has cared for them, he has never harmed any, not even by mistake but he can't stand anyone who hurts an animal.

There used to be a farmer who would bring his sheep to some now disused shearing sheds near here. Sometimes, to shear, mules, or separate the lambs from the mothers, something I always find unendurable. They respond as any mother would to their child being taken away, and their little lambs cry as our children do. When Billy heard the mothers and babies crying, he would pace the fence, roaring with rage. Though I understood how Billy felt, I realised I had to put Billy in a yard when the farmer came.

Billy responds to animals being hurt and the loss of his friends with emotions I have witnessed no other animal express. Once, a goat of ours died. It had only just passed and was lying on the ground while we worked out where to bury it. When Billy saw his dead friend, he became inconsolable. He ran around his dead body, kicking up the dirt, bellowing with a grief that was so agonising it sounded as if it had tapped into a well of trauma that wound back through every living being that had ever walked this earth. We could only step back and give him time to grieve.

I often see Billy as a wise and noble warrior for Mother Nature. He is a gentle giant around energies that harmonise and respect our planet, but he can stir like a sleeping volcano around the cruel and greedy or those who plunder our earth for their own gain. It is better for him and less noble others if we keep him away from more plunderous activities and let him spend his time in nature living in a gentle and holy way as he shepherds his beloveds, our sheep.

Just recently, he turned up at the fence around our home. He does visit periodically; after all, Gill and I are his mum and dad, or the only ones he has ever known. He is very affectionate and loves to lick us as if we are lollipops, but the ferocity and passion of his licks

feel like being put through an industrial cheese grater-
they are lethal. But during this last visit, something was
different- something felt wrong, and we couldn't understand what Billy was trying to communicate. He was very
vocal and kept trying to get our attention. Then, in the
distance, we noticed a sheep walking as if she couldn't
see. When we went over to check her out, we realised
she was blind. Billy had brought her home, and that was
what he was trying to tell us. She needed looking after
and would not survive out in the bush with the others.
As soon as the sheep was safe with us, he left. He had
done what he'd come to do - Mission accomplished.

We decided to bring a couple of other sheep home to
keep this blind girl company, and Billy often brings his
tribe in for visits. I love watching him walk down the
track to our home, his herd of woolly friends following
behind. Most people around us fail to understand why
we choose not to profit financially from such a huge
majestic bull. I am told he is worth a lot of money, but
no financial reward could ever compensate for the loss
of this feeling and sensitive creature from our lives. The
gift his presence brings to our lives is our gold.

And when I go for a walk with our dogs and, I come
across Billy and his tribe sitting under the shade of a
tree. Our earthy and caring King in the midst of his
soft and gentle woolly friends, I feel so blessed. It's
as if I have slipped into an enchanted reality where
animals can choose their friends and their lives, and

there are no barriers to love. A place of such peace and harmony, it is perfectly normal for a prized bull to live a long, love-filled life, and where sheep no longer suffer hardships for our greed or our palate. A place of such gentleness that their treasured babies are as loved and cherished as ours.

In these moments, I realise that here, where the wounded and unwanted of the animal kingdom gather, we are already living this wonderful reality, and together, we are holding space for all those who have yet to find this place of abiding LOVE.

Part of Billy's story is from 'Sacred Journey into the Animal Realms'

Twenty-Four

Baalu & his Herd

Y ou should see our beautiful Orla. She shines so red she looks as if she has been cast from sunshine and embers. I love watching her frolic around the paddock; tail held high in the air as she daintily prances, looking like the Arabian princess she had never been- until now.

Orla was a rescue, and, like many rescue operations, this one did not work out as expected.

We'd had a call about five horses that needed a home. Like so many rescue jobs, there was an ultimatum- if they failed to find a home, they would be shot. No one had any photos of them, so we offered to do the two-hour drive, take as many photos as we could, and get more details that would aid us in finding this small group, a home.

We arrived on a wet day, and these poor horses looked so mournful as they stood knee-deep in mud in a small yard. While a couple of them were thin, three of the horses were skeletal. Their owner had died and left behind a lot of horses that were roaming around the small local community trying to find food. The country was in a drought; cattle everywhere were dying, people were struggling to feed their sheep, and there was no food. Some of the prettier horses had already been stolen, and some had been hit by cars and killed. The local police officer who loved animals was determined to find them all homes, but she only had a small amount of time to do so. They would be shot if they were still in the yards in a week.

While there were five horses, one was a stallion, and we were told a local man wanted to keep him. I certainly felt sad he would be separated from his tribe, but it would make rehoming the others easier.

We took our photos, returned home, and began to put out for the perfect home. We had a small horse truck and were even willing to deliver them. I was so happy when we secured a home for them with a woman experienced in handling horses who lived on acreage. They would be well looked after, and it was a great outcome.

With less than a week before the horses had to be moved from their yards, we organised to deliver them in four days. Somehow, we had pulled off a miracle, and the horses would be relocated in time, but the day before Gill was due to deliver them, this woman pulled out due to personal reasons. It was deeply disappointing. Gill had spent several days servicing our truck to prepare it for the six-hour trip.

The only option left to avoid them being shot was to bring them all home. We were experiencing drought too; our paddocks were dustbowls, and the cost of hay had soared with the price of gold, but somehow, we would work it out. We always trusted in our path, and even though we often lived life on the edge, we felt looked after. *We can do this*, we agreed.

While Gill was away picking up the horses, I spent the day getting our yards ready. When I finally heard the sound of our truck coming up our driveway, I ran out, eager to meet our new friends. I could hear the steamy impatience of the horses in the back, keen to get out. It was then Gill told me he had an extra gift; the stallion was in there as well. The man who'd claimed him had decided he didn't want him eithur.

Unexpectedly, I felt relieved at this news; I had seen this horses bond with his girls and how protective he was. I'd had an aching heart all day at the thought of them being taken away from him while he was left on his own. Oh, I know that sometimes keeping the animals together is often a luxury most can't afford, but we must when we can.

Most of the horses were so thin their skin was shrunken like leather over their ribs. When we had stood in the rain the first time we saw them, sloshing through the mud to get better photos, they had looked as if their life force had been sucked from them. They had felt so beaten they were beyond even desperation. As I watched them come down the horse ramp and explore their huge yard, the sun had finally begun to shine. While they still looked worn down from life, there was an ember of a new feeling: hope.

It appeared that the red mare we called Queenie was pregnant. Her belly bulged unnaturally from her shrunken body. We knew we would have to do everything we could to support her through her pregnancy so her foal stood the best chance of surviving.

By the time the spring came and Queenie gave birth, the horses were all blooming. The week before her birth, I'd had a dream that the foal was Holy and had its own divine purpose, and its name was Mahran. I had no idea if the foal was a male or female, but I was convinced it was a filly; something about the dream had felt so feminine.

I did not know Queenie's past, but something had evidently traumatised her; she has always had a deep mistrust of people. I have tried so many routes with this older girl, and none have had a harvest, so now I just let her be. And because I did not want to cause her any stress, I watched her newborn foal, a little chestnut with white socks and long lanky legs, from a distance. I had been so convinced she would give birth to a filly that I hadn't even checked the sex of the foal. I announced to all our supporters that Queenie had birthed a girl.

When Gill later told me it was a colt, I didn't believe him. I had to see for myself. There was no doubting the evidence. He was right; it was indeed a boy!

But boy or girl, it didn't matter; Maha, as we affectionally called him, was beautiful. I was so awed by how close his life as an unborn foal had danced on the edge of death. Not only from his mother's skeletal condition, but he could have been shot, and maybe that is why he had such a zest for life. He galloped everywhere at such speed he was always getting scratched by branches, cutting himself or grazing his knees as he fell. We were constantly cleaning his numerous cuts, hoping the scar on his face would heal, praying he would slow down; at this rate, he would never make old age.

Fortunately, unlike his mum, he was born with a consuming curiosity to get to know us, and when he was only a few days old, had wobbled over to us on his long lanky legs. I love these horses with a passion. I was so glad we had stretched beyond how many animals we felt we could nurture through a drought because we did it. Under our care, these horses bloomed.

And the stallion, well, it was rumoured that the old man who'd died had a stallion that was worth a lot of money, but no one knew which one. Many of his stallions had been taken by those greedy for cash, and they had left only one- our Baluu, named after the moon in the local aboriginal dialect Yulararyway.

As he regained his weight, his entire dun-coloured coat changed colour. Once, I shared a photo of him prancing around the paddock. He shone with so much health his coat looked gold and was speckled with all these appaloosa markings. Now, I do not know anything about horse breeds or colouring; the superficial stuff is interesting, but beyond a mild curiosity, I want to get to know their soul. When some horsey people who follow our sanctuary contacted me and told me to be cautious sharing photos of such a valuable horse, *You don't want him to be stolen;* I wondered if we had indeed got the gold. I hoped so because an animal's monetary value was unimportant to us; we were not selling, and we would not be making money from him for breeding.

It has been several years since this group joined our tribe, and other horses have arrived since then. Some had been kept in a small yard for over ten years and were depressed and thin and shrunken. Within weeks, they were splashing in our river, sleeping under the stars, and roaming like wild brumbies across the plains. I loved witnessing that haunted look they had in their eyes when they first arrived, fade away and be replaced with a sparkling joy for life.

The drought finally broke, and it rained so much that the water pooled and made so many shallow ponds that became home to ducks and frogs and mosquitos. Sometimes, a blessing can have a hidden curse; we prayed for the rain but did not anticipate being bitten alive. All our animals were uncomfortable. The chickens were constantly twitching and fidgeting on their perches, the pigs grunted with discomfort, and the horses were endlessly twitching their tails and irritably lifting their feet.

So began the time of the big smokey fires; we lit them every night before the sun went down and the mozzies came out. We lit lots of little smouldering, smokey fires in big tin buckets and had them burning all around our sanctuary in an attempt to protect as many animals as we could and smoke the mozzies out. We would start with some kindling and wood in the bottom of the bucket and fill them with leaves and camel poop, and anything we thought would create a pungent smoke to keep the little biters away. The pigs had a fire each, Bella our donkey had one, and she would stand right over the top of her bucket with her head in the smoke; there was no way she was getting bitten. We also had smokey fires lit in amongst the chickens so they could get some sleep. Out the front of our home, where the larger animals grazed, we lit two enormous fires for the other animals.

Each day, Gill would drive out and gather a trailer full of wood for the night's giant smudging ceremony. The animals soon realised that if they hung around the fires, they were mostly mozzie-free.

These fires began to feel like a holy happening. In the midst of animal agriculture, where every animal is only valued for financial gain, something magnificent and beautiful was happening here. Each night, animals would arrive to sit around the fire. We often went out after dark to toss more wood and leaves and poop on the flames so the fires would smoke throughout the night. Sitting around the fire in deep contentment and peace would be camels, sheep, and goats. Our giant bull, Billy Beloved, was also there, as were Spirit and his wee ponies and Orla, Queenie, and little Maha. All sitting together under the moon and the stars, each one silhouetted by the flames of the fires.

Gill and I often laughed when we tried to imagine what the farmers thought as they drove past. They already thought we were deranged, caring for so many animals without a thought of profit. We could imagine them shaking their heads in consternation, wondering if they were hallucinating- camels, horses, and all sorts of animals, sitting around a massive campfire. Flames leaping high into the night sky. Oh, I know that many would not have understood the love we live in, but as they drove past, I did hope just a little of our love, rubbed off.

Twenty-Five

Treasure Trail

O racle was a green and pink princess parrot, and I first saw her advertised for sale on Facebook for $200. She was sitting in an empty and bleak cage, and the despair I felt from her hit me so hard I knew I had to help her. I decided to ask my Facebook friends if anyone wanted to help me raise the $200. If our supporters could help me buy her, she could come and live with us. Within ten seconds, a beautiful soul had offered to pay the money.

At the speed of light, I wrote SOLD underneath the post. I was jubilant that we had manifested the money, and this parrot would soon be in a loving home. I nearly fell off my chair in surprise when the reply came that she had already been sold.

I sat in disbelief

This had to be wrong. My feeling to help this parrot had felt so strong. Surely, he would send me another message telling me he'd got it wrong and this bird had not been sold. I waited in anticipation, but no reply came. I didn't want to harass the man, but I was carrying out the Universe's bidding. I was a woman on a divine mission. I messaged the seller again and asked him if he was sure.

His answer was the same, but he told me he had two budgies for sale for $20 if I wanted them. I didn't really want any budgies, but I could feel the enticing lure of a treasure trail, so I agreed.

 While Gill drove into town to collect our new and somewhat unexpected budgies, I prepared their aviary. It was a big space; there was an area open to the weather where many plants grew, with a small pond. I knew these birds would be thrilled. They could fly, bathe in the rain or splash in their own pond.

I didn't know how long Gill would be, so I decided to go for a walk with our dogs. The land we lived on was so beautiful that often I would stand in the garden- just for a moment as I had work to do, then all of a sudden, a magnetic pull too strong to resist would lure me out into the bush. I would walk for hours exploring the foliage that grew on the edge of the lake, gathering sap from the ancient trees and stopping to pick up feathers and magical stones. Nature was irresistible, and I always came home restored. Often, I would bump into animals we had cared for; some would even join me on my walk. Having an emu join me, or a kangaroo we had once hand-reared wasn't unusual. I love that deep connection I felt with nature where even the wild animals knew us.

By the time I got home from this day's walk, Gill had already put our new budgies in the aviary. I was a little disappointed it had happened without me; I had been so excited to see their response to their new surroundings. I had hung branches of gum leaves, and there was a bowl of fruit; I wanted them to feel so welcomed. I ran to the aviary and got the most beautiful surprise. There, sitting on a perch, were two budgies and a Princess Parrot. *What happened?* I asked excitedly. Apparently, the person who'd agreed to buy her had not turned up Gill told me. I was so happy; I should have trusted I had known she was meant to come to us.

Only later, as we watched these three birds preen and nestle each other, did we understand what had oc- curred. The love between these birds was palpable. They had lived in bleak cages in the same yard. Their comfort had been each other. Oracle's partner had died in the heat in a cage with no shade. The fact that any of these birds had survived their loveless and uncared-for life was miraculous, but their desire to help each other and remain together had been so strong that the Uni- verse had conspired to help them. They all wanted to escape their old home but it had to be together. If I had purchased Oracle immediately, I would not have known about her two friends -the budgies, Tutti and Sky. The three of them were inseparable, and just sitting in their abode and soaking up the gentle fairy-like energy they each emanated was like spending time in a holy temple; I always felt renewed.

So often, when you care for animals, it can be hard, heartbreaking and exhausting. This is all a part of doing this work, but these moments of blissed-out reunion when something so beautiful happens to lift three creatures from the direst of homes, this nourishes us, keeps us going, fills us with so much love, we have space in our hearts for the next creature in need.

We had other birds we were caring for, too. I had turned our huge vegetable garden, which was covered in fruit netting to protect it from the chooks, into our biggest aviary and inside, was yet another holy and magnificent experience.

For many years, we had cared for all sorts of wildlife, and the bubs who had taken over our vegetable garden were two of my absolute favourites.

Olly Tosh was a frog-mouth owl who had come to us when he was only a few days old, and Silver was an orphaned kestrel. It was a really big space with numerous perches. At one end was a pet carrier that was Silvers abode, and the place where I fed him his already dead mice. Even as a tiny bird, he would mantle over his food, hissing and spitting, if I came near. These birds of prey are so focused and streamlined that their energy has the dynamism of an electrical charge. While I adored looking after Silver, I was very aware he was a wild little bird with deadly talons that could hurt me.

The most cruisey little bub, Ollie, was at the other end of the enclosed garden. He was laid back and gentle, loved to play and would often tug on a stick in the hope I would tussle with him, which I did. I was surprised by this. I don't know if you have ever seen a Frog mouth owl in the wild, but they sit like little statues, and their perfectly hued feathers blend in and make them look like a branch. They can be hard to spot in the wild and are not known for their boisterous play. In fact they are not known for moving much at all.

I am so used to interspecies connections and animals of all different kinds living together in harmony, so sometimes I don't think about any issues. However, some in our wildlife group worried about the dynamic between a diurnal bird and one that was nocturnal. An expert they contacted advised me to separate these birds immediately. Fortunately, I had the support of a remarkable woman in our group who dealt with birds. She trusted my judgement and told me to do what felt right. I was grateful for this but felt a little shaken by the advice I had been given. *What if have made a big mistake?* I rushed to the veggie garden to find Silver and Ollie sitting on a branch together so peacefully; my self-doubt was the only friction in this harmonious haven. I backed out and watched them from outside for ages before dismissing the idea of separation.

I had put them in an ample space together because they were babies; it's not normal for any baby to be alone. Yes, they were a different species, but in the wild, they most likely would be no threat to each other. I didn't know; I had only done what felt right, and it was working. And in all the time they coexisted in our garden, I did not experience a single problem. These two bubs were friends.

One day, I was working in the veggie garden, clearing out some weeds, and Ollie flew towards me and landed on my shoulder. He often landed on me, but this time I could see Silver at the far end of the garden and he was watching intently. A look passed across his face, telling me he had just realised he was missing out. There were other perks to having a human mum. He took off from his perch and landed on my other shoulder. There was Ollie on one side, Silver on the other, and me, Mum, in the middle.

They grew up being able to fly from an early age, so by the time they were ready for release, they both flew strongly. For a month or two, they would both visit separately. I always left Ollie his homemade beetle balls, which I made especially for him, full of dead insects and everything he loved. With Silver, I would go outside at sunset and call his name. I would outstretch my arm, and in my hand, I held a dead mouse. Silver could hear me from far away, and he would come flying towards me, dipping and diving at such speed. That last moment before he grabbed the mouse was terrifying and thrilling. It was like standing in the precise spot where lightning was about to strike and knowing it was about to hit. Watching his outstretched talons as he swooped down towards me, tearing through the air with such speed and grace, then, at the last moment, he would grab the mouse and fly off-his wild shrieks piercing the air.

The lessons of the animals and perhaps life are always the same- Trust in yourselves, listen to the voice within and let go of all your doubts. I have had this lesson over and over again, and it has become easier. Each time I witness my deep knowing manifest, even if it took a different route to bring Oracle and her beloved budgie friends to us or the friendship and harmony that developed between two birds with different rhythms and currents, I do trust more.

In many ways, trusting in ourselves can mean we are more likely to go against the tide or veer away from well-worn tracks because what guides us does not come from workshops or books. It's a holy voice that speaks to us from within, and the more I trust this wise and loving guidance, the more harmony the animals and I live in.

Twenty-Six

The Colonel & his Wish

The first rooster I ever loved was a huge Rhode Island Red with a bright red cone and feathers, the colours of sweet chestnut conkers. Not only was he my first love, but he was also my first experience of a rooster. Even though we were offering him an escape from his owner's intentions to turn him into a chicken curry, we spent three days chasing him all over the place in an attempt to catch him. He did not want to be caught. Finally, Gill made a big, bold dash and caught him.

I sympathised and recognised my own resistance in the chase around the farmer's yards. I have often kicked and screamed at what has inevitably become my good fortune. It's often hard to see beyond the disguise of the moment and recognise what's truly going on. I am sure he would have eagerly jumped into our arms if he had known his life would transform with big adventures, girls, and more love than he'd ever known. Instead, he saw two people chasing him, and that brought up every fear. People had always been predators, and he was their prey, only it was different this time.

Over the years, I had heard so many horrendous tales of people being chased by roosters, who became too terrified to set foot outside in case their rooster attacked them- but this majestic creature was not at all like that.

He had the proud dignity of one born to command, and I could easily imagine him marching proudly at the front of a military procession, medals pinned to his feathered chest. His name was obvious; this was The Colonel.

As he sat on my lap being cuddled all the way home, I think it sunk in that life had taken a drastic turn. He soon settled into his new chook home with his nine gorgeous girls and immediately became their dashing and honourable protector.

For over a year, he wandered our five acres with his happy tribe and never ever ventured onto our veranda. That was until my partner Gill and I began to plan our big adventure of travelling through the desert with our camels. Gill had already begun building the wagon our camels would pull, and while it was almost complete, it awaited the final touches we couldn't do until we freed up some money and sold the house.

One morning, The Colonel climbed onto our veranda, and despite trying to entice him back to his lovely home with all his girls, he sat on the back of an armchair and would not budge - for three days. We had no idea why he had suddenly left his girls. We had never seen him behave like this before. *Was he sick?* He looked healthy, *but what on earth was wrong?* He was adamant he was not leaving; I was deeply curious as to why he had swayed from his guardianship of his girls to hang out on one of our two chairs. Those two comfy armchairs were our retreat and relaxation from our busy days, planning our desert trip while finishing renovations, running a business and caring for numerous camels in various states of health.

With the addition of a huge copper fireplace purchased from our tip shop, Gill had transformed our cold veranda into an enticing place to sit on a cold winter's night. As we planned and plotted and dreamt of escape, The Colonel sat clucking beside us. Sometimes, I surprise myself by how slow I am in understanding the communication of our animals. All of a sudden, I understood. I had no idea why it had taken so long or how I had been so obtuse. *The Colonel wanted to come on the trip and travel with us in the camel wagon!*

Wow, of course, he could come. It had not occurred to us before to take our chickens, but we were open about how our trip would unfold. I'd presumed we would find them a fantastic home, but after that light bulb moment, we began to look at all our animals differently. The doves could come too. We could also hang our parrot's cages from the wagon. The Colonel had expanded our horizons and opened us up to possibilities we had never even imagined. When we happily reassured him he could come, he clucked contentedly, left the veranda and returned home.

Gill immediately began building a home for the chickens in the wagon and then one for the doves. The Noah's Ark of animals that was to join us had begun.

While I loved viewing every step in the wagon's progress, I didn't like walking through Gill's workspace. I had no idea how he created such practical beauty from the spew of rusty razor-edged chaos he worked in where one trip and you could get tetanus or splice open a vein. And yet he did; our wagon was not only sturdy enough for the roughest terrain, but it had the graceful curves of a boat.

The Colonels's new travelling abode was built between the two giant front wheels and stretched under the belly of the wagon halfway back. The front was mesh so the chickens could sit inside their home and watch the world go by as we travelled. At the back were their nesting boxes that we could access easily from the outside. Gill had made a ladder so the chickens could climb into their house and a beautiful tool that would make cleaning them out much more accessible. It had a long handle, and you could reach the back of their home and scrape all their bedding out. Everything he made was a work of art and had its own special place in the wagon.

When we finally reached the point of teaching The Colonel and his girls how to get in the wagon, we placed bales of hay on each side of the ladder. Every night, they jumped on the hay-bales and climbed back into their home. After a week, we took the bales away, and by this time, they were so used to their new home they shimmied up the ladder.

I had never given much thought to the challenges of travelling with a rooster. There was one sheet of metal between us and his early morning crows. At first, we nearly jumped out of our skins in fright. To be woken at 3 am by a series of Cock-A-Doodle-Doos so deafening our feathered love could have been sleeping on the pillow beside us was like being in a pilot's ejector seat. One minute, we were in the deepest, most dreamy sleep; the next, bolt upright awake, and there was no going back.

But we loved The Colonel; we were sure we would work it out, and we did.

I had never lived so closely with so many animals before. Every day, we were together all the time, through dust-storms, wind and hale, through thunder and fire-light, beauty and pain. It was as if we all began to pulse in this symbiotic relationship with each other. Our various rhythms and currents began to adjust to one another, and that could be the outcome of accepting each other. Somehow, despite the differences or the challenges, we all began to unify in harmony. The fact we no longer jumped out of our skins at The Colonel's dawn chorus crept up on us. We would realise we had slept like two contented cherubs all the way through

There were aspects of our chickens we had never considered; they kept every place we camped free from scorpions and centipedes. If they saw one, they ate it. They loved travelling too. Each morning, we would feed and water them before leaving for our daily journey in the camel wagon. After breakfast, they would cluckily make themselves comfy, tussling one another to get the best seat in the front of their pen. They all loved travelling and wanted the best view of the road. We averaged about six kilometres an hour, slow enough to gather all sorts of edibles the chickens loved. I always felt like the ice cream lady in the cinema when I threw their treats in. I often saw them sitting happily in beds of golden flowers.

We always made a point of pulling up for the day and making camp by mid-afternoon. That way, the chickens had plenty of time to come out and explore. Bedtime, they went back in to their home, until mid-afternoon the following day. Other camel wagon travellers have told me their chickens didn't lay eggs. Ours laid plenty, but they were happy; their care was as focused and attentive as it was for our dogs and camels.

I once heard some wisdom from an old farmer who told us you always travel at the pace of the slowest animal.

We always did this. Every life was important, and their well-being was a priority. Without the chickens, we may have travelled more kilometres in a day, but with them, we maintained a healthy balance and didn't totally exhaust ourselves each day.

The Colonel lived a life that few roosters have ever experienced. He was so dear to me, and long after our wagon pulled up and we began to create a new home, he always had a special place in our hearts and often sat beside our fire inside, especially in Winter. As he got old and more frail and sensitive to the extremes of life, he lived with us at our hearth. He would sit on a dog bed in front of the fire, just like one of the dogs.

The moment he left this life, I was holding him in my arms, telling him how we loved him and how special he was. For me, he was always a wise sage and a wizard.

Animals have shown me so many times that our bodies are only an illusion. So often, we fail to see the true being inside the body because we get stuck on the veneer. We may have called him The Colonel, but we saw beyond that- we saw the soul and that divine spark of infinite love that unites us all.

And who knows, somewhere in the chicken house right now, an egg may be hatching, and it could even be our highly esteemed and utterly adorable friend, The Colonel, back to share another wild camel adventure.

Twenty-Seven

Yumyum & his Maiden Flight

Y umyum, our man attacking Galah, had settled well into his new life with us and *loved* travelling in our wagon. We'd been told by his previous owners he couldn't fly, so we always let him out whenever we stopped and camped. Often, he would sit on the back of my chair as we sat around our campfire. He was such a character, but he was also a little rotter, and we had to set clear boundaries for him.

He became so possessive when he hung out inside our wagon. If Gill or I tried to enter, he would fly at us in full attack mode. It was funny and terrifying at the same time because his bite *really* hurt. Once, so much noise was coming from inside our wagon that I stood on our huge front wheel to look inside. I was trying to be as quiet as I could. The prospect of him seeing me was chilling. While surreptitiously peeping, I watched him frog marching across our bed like a mini dictator, tossing anything he didn't want on the bed onto the floor. When he saw me watching him, he gave me such an evil look. In my absolute haste to get away, I stepped backward off the wheel and landed on the earth in a laughing, shaking heap.

He was so ferocious he left us no choice but to *ban* him from our home unless he was safely in his cage. As we travelled, he saw more action from his cage in a day than most caged birds experience in a lifetime, and he loved it. He'd screech with excitement, share our food, try and grab leaves from the trees when they brushed his cage, and he was always a very vocal member of the pre-wagon rolling chorus.

Every morning, as we gave that first command to our camels to *pullem up*, our big ark-like wagon would lurch forward into the day with every dog and parrot howling and screeching loudly. They were so excited and made an almighty din. I would have preferred a far less rowdy start to the day, but nothing worked to shut them up.-a nd believe me, we tried!

We had been travelling through a landscape that was so dry and hot, and when we arrived at an unexpected waterhole about a kilometre long, we decided to take a well-earned break.

Giant old gum trees lined the creek, their branches full of noisy galahs. Wild ducks were bobbing and diving in the water, making it look so enticing and brightly coloured parrots I'd not seen before flitted from tree to tree. Even though the summery heat had begun to wane and the days were edged with cold, we had travelled through drought and heat for so long that I felt as if I had arrived in heaven. I couldn't wait to get into the water and bob around with the ducks, but first, we took all the camels down to the water's edge for a drink.

Many of our camels thought water came in buckets and were experiencing a waterhole for the first time.

I sat on the giant roots of an ancient gum tree that grew on the sandy banks of the river's shore and watched our beautiful herd of camels approach the water in an excited huddle—inching their way nervously down to the water's edge until they got too scared. Then, with a big kick and a buck, they'd all cavort back across the sandy beach to the safety of the river's bank. Then, gaining more courage and becoming more intrepid, they cautiously walked down to the water's edge again, testing out the soft sand that made them nervous when they sunk almost to their ankles. They had many practice attempts before they were brave enough to drink from the water. Finally satiated, they began to kick and jump playfully in the shallows, showering sprays of sunlight sparkling water everywhere. Big red Alice boldly walked deeper than the rest, sat down and began to roll, which encouraged a few more of them to sit down and roll. Soon, the water was a writhing mass of camels rolling and splashing. Their wet bodies looked golden in the sunlight. I watched, intoxicated by the life I was living. So raw and free that every breath I took felt lurid and ripe with life. I felt this massive release of energy as I watched them having so much fun. We'd all been working hard, and we deserved this break.

I felt really peaceful as I walked back to our camp and was utterly unprepared for Yumyum's death-defying heroics. We had left our flightless cocky sitting happily on the back of a chair, but he was nowhere to be seen. We checked everywhere in camp and were just extending our worried search to the surrounding bushes when we heard him screeching excitedly from *above* us. He was flying! Flying like he'd *never* done before. He was doing big raucous show-off laps around our wagon, apparently, just as surprised as we were that he could fly. As he flew through the air, he was making so much noise every hungry hawk could hear him, and it didn't take long before I noticed a falcon take off from the highest branches of a nearby tree. This predator was so fast and deadly that Yumyum didn't stand a chance.

The falcon sliced through the air straight towards our little Galah on his maiden flight. Yet Yumyum put on the performance of his life. He was dipping, diving and swerving so fast as he tried to outfly this hungry falcon who was always an inch away from his tail. I watched this encounter, unable to breathe, and felt utterly sick. There was nothing we could do to help our little parrot. Yet, miraculously, he made it to safety within the leafy foliage of an old gum tree.

Anxious that my little bird would take off again and put himself back in danger, I ran to the tree. I saw Yumyum high up on a branch, almost hidden amongst the leaves. His heart must have been beating so fast I could see from the ground; his body was shaking. I knew he'd be safe in the tree but wanted him home. My legs were still shaking, and I felt weak from the shock of watching our cheeky little mutt of a bird in such danger. I couldn't even think about relaxing until he was safely *in* his cage, yet each time I called him, he ignored me.

Confident that if I gave him some time to calm down, he'd come, and not wanting to leave him unattended, I sat at the bottom of the tree and waited. Gill even bought me a cup of tea. I kept talking to Yumyum, telling him we just wanted to take him home, but an hour passed, and he was still sitting there, ignoring every attempt I made to entice him down.

For the rest of the day, I sat under the tree and by the time the sun began to set, he was still high up in the branches and out of reach from us. I had no choice but to leave him for the night. My only consolation was he wouldn't try and fly in the dark. Well, I didn't think he would, anyway.

I got up early with high expectations of being reunited with my little mate, but the day continued in the same way. I stood at the bottom of the tree with food and water for him, trying to lure my usually adoring little chum down, but still, he acted as if I wasn't even there. He didn't even look down. I was calling him. I even sang to him but didn't even get a curious glance. He was way up high. So high Gill couldn't even climb the tree to get him down. My only choice was to wait until he chose to come down himself and pray he didn't fly off somewhere else and put himself in danger again. He looked fine. I even watched him stripping some leaves from the branches with his beak. He was in his own little world, and we didn't exist!

It wasn't until day three of my vigil at the bottom of the tree that Gill came up with an idea. By this time, I had my own little settlement, complete with books and drinks and a fire pit for brewing tea, so I didn't have to leave the Yumyum tree. Gill flopped down beside me laughingly and told me to follow his lead. Wrapping his arms around me, he began kissing me passionately on my lips.

It took all of ten seconds. Yumyum flew down from that tree like a kamikaze pilot ready to tear into Gill and would have clawed and bitten him if Gill hadn't swiftly gotten out of the way. I was astounded we hadn't thought of this before. Yumyum always bristled when Gill got close to me.

I wrapped my little parrot safely in a towel with his head sticking out, something he *loved* and nestled him like a baby. He chuckled happily as I carried him back to the safety of his cage. I could finally relax.

Yumyum had done the impossible, not only flown when he never had before, in his unfit condition he had also outflown a bird of prey. Oh my, it had been an emotionally fraying few days. *My goodness, aren't you a hero?* I said to him as he danced along his perch. He was back, but he was different. His chest looked plumped up with pride, but it was more than that. A shift so subtle that I only noticed because we lived every moment as we travelled, together. Before, there had been a hollowness, as if he was only the shell of his wild self, which certainly explained his aggression. Happy people don't hurt others, and happy parrots do not bite. While affectionate with women, he bit every man within range, including Gill. The previous owner's husband had given his wife an ultimatum- the parrot or me. And while Gill had gone through his battles with him and been chased around our camp, we both believed this wounded little parrot would get better.

In a place of love, everything heals. It has to. Energy always moves to harmonise with the highest frequency, and it was only a matter of time.

I had been so absorbed in Yumyums safety I hadn't considered how his death-defying feat would impact him. His previous sad life had been lived for people's entertainment, dancing manically on his perch in a dance-cocky-rant, or chasing the menfolk while everyone laughed. And what they had laughed at was a broken and wounded bird's trauma and suffering.

Yumyum had never had a chance to do anything wild and reckless and brave and magnificent before. He had never sat at the top of a tall tree as the leaves rustled and danced in sunlight and wind, with other birds, just like him, landing in the branches beside him. I'd felt sick with anguish as I'd watched him tear through the sky, dipping and diving as he fought for his life, but I hadn't realised that as Yumyum crossed the threshold from domesticity to the wild, he was reclaiming his life and he was taking back his power. Our little bird had changed, and it was for the better.

We were all transforming on this trip. I had always anticipated I would grow, but I had underestimated how every animal with us would also free themselves from the shackles of the past and become braver, happier, calmer, and more trusting in life-just as we were.

Adapted from 'Tracks of Love'

Twenty-Eight

Beautiful & Charlie

S ome days, the challenges of travelling with so many
animals were just never-ending. All I wanted to do
was bake a fruit cake in the camp oven and, when it was
cooked, sit down by the fire with a cup of Earl Grey
tea. Just the thought had me sighing with relief. We'd
come a long way since self-medicating on fags or the
days when I still had a home, and I'd comfort eat blocks
of chocolate or get drunk on red wine. My hard-old life
on the road had obviously given me some harmony.

I was just mixing up all the ingredients for my cake
when a couple of corellas flew screeching above us
before circling our wagon. This was odd behaviour for
wild parrots, and Gill and I surmised they'd come
to say hello to our two corellas, Beautiful and Charlie. When I went to see how they were responding, I was
shocked to see their cage door was wide open. These
two birds *were* Beautiful, and Charlie and that worried
me.

In the two years since we'd had them, we'd never handled them. I had no idea how we would catch them

again. Since we'd left on the trip, they'd become much more communicative and connected to us. They were our constant companions in the front of the wagon, and we regularly played with them. Their favourite game was a tug of war with a stick, and they would tussle and tug at it like excited little puppies. But neither of them had any experience in the wild. While Charlie was confident taking new steps, Beautiful was timid and would often hide behind him. She'd lived for so long in a tiny cage that her confidence had been stripped.

I put my unbaked cake aside.

There wasn't much light left in the quickly darkening cerise-streaked sky and Charlie, eager to explore, took off flying along the dry creek bed with Lovely following him. Cake long forgotten, we traipsed after them as they flew from one big old gum tree to the next. It was almost dark when we saw Beautiful land on a really low branch. Between us, we managed to catch her in a towel. She looked pleased to be wrapped up safely as we carried home.

Charlie flew back with us, and while we couldn't catch him, he did at least sleep on the wagon's roof, which gave me some peace. At least I knew where he was.

My mantra for the next two days, in between mouthfuls of the cake I'd finally managed to bake, was *Let go, Kye and enjoy*. Who was I to rush the experience of a little parrot who'd finally flown free for the first time in several decades? Once again, it was a lesson in letting go to each moment and not racing ahead.

Something extraordinary was unfolding in our lopsided camp in amongst the shale, and Charlie's first flight was important. Momentous even. He had lived constricted for so long, and he was birthing a new reality for himself that was so liberating I had tears in my eyes as he soared through the air, screeching with joy. And just like Yumyum, he *really* strutted his stuff when he landed on the wagon. He was fluffed up with pride and so happy at his new-found capabilities that despite the discomfort of our camp, I had the biggest smile.

With all his new-found joy, I did worry a little we wouldn't be able to catch him. He showed no interest in his cage or Beautiful, but on the third day, he landed beside her and wanted to get back in. His little mate was delighted. She'd paced anxiously without him, and the two cuddled up, preening each other. I breathed a *huge* sigh of relief we'd got him. One more sleep, and we could finally leave our stony and inhospitable haven.

I had no idea then that Charlie's unexpected adventure would change his life forever.

Several months later, our nomadic entourage pulled in at a homestead we had agreed to rent over the summer. We had no intention of risking the well-being of our animals by travelling through extreme heat. When the cooler weather returned our journey would continue.

Knowing we would be stationary for several months, we turned the framework of the big water tank outside into an aviary for Beautiful and Charlie. It was a huge high space, and I could tell Beautiful was content. However, Charlie, since the day he had flown all around the wagon, wanted more. His yearning for the wild was palpable, and while I wanted him to have his freedom, I didn't know how to do this without Beautiful being left alone. I should have known we can never work these things out with our heads, though we can ask to be shown the perfect way. And what happened was far more perfect than anything I could have imagined or thought up.

Down in the gully, giant gum trees lined the dry creek bed that only flowed in flood. With all their nooks and hollows, these trees provided the perfect environment for nesting parrots. Hundreds of corellas lived and nested in them. They were so noisy we could hear them from the house, and they had evidently heard the calls of Charlie and Beautiful. Every day, they flew up to their aviary and hung out with them. We had Corellas sitting in all the trees and on the fence posts around the house. This went on for weeks, and those birds didn't miss a day. Of course, I could feel Charlie's frustration building, but I could also sense that whatever unfolded would do so in its own time.

Then, one day, I came out, and the latch on the door of the aviary had come undone. Charlie had gone.

Beautiful was anxious and calling out for her mate. I tried to reassure her, but she was very agitated, and I was so relieved when Charlie returned. He had all his new mates with him, and they all sat around the aviary. Charlie looked as if he was talking to Beautiful. She sat on a perch next to the wire. Her head was so close to Charlie's. It was easy to imagine what he was saying to Beautiful.

Come on, Beautiful, we can have the life we were meant to live now. We were never meant to be in cages. Imagine how you will feel as we soar through the sky in our flock. Come on, Beautiful, come with me.

Each night, Charlie would leave with his flock, a wild bird now. Beautiful, would pace and call out for him, and it would be like that until he returned in the morning. Since Charlie had got out, I had left the aviary door wide open. Both these parrots were free to do as they pleased. This was their life, not mine, and whatever they were working out, they just needed a safe haven and time.

Then, one morning, I went out to feed Beautiful, and she was gone. I am such a worrisome mum. *Would she cope, would she get anxious?* She was such a nervous little bird, but I felt sure her nerves had come from being forced into a life that wasn't natural. Life in a cage had disconnected her from the purity of her own wild expression. I would soon see this was the truth.

It took a couple of days for them to return, and I wept with joy seeing Beautiful's excitement. They were both screeching with delight as they flew laps of the house before taking off again with their mates to the giant gum trees in the dry creek bed. I was happy and sad. Sad to see my dear friends go but so intrinsically delighted that I wept with joy that these two precious little beings had reclaimed the life that was theirs. It was an outcome I had never anticipated, and it was perfect.

They often visited during the next few months, but the space between visits slowly decreased. I felt so grateful it had happened like that. Their visits had shown me they were both OK and that I didn't need to worry. The love we shared was real. They knew I loved them enough to let them go, and I felt their love and gratitude.

Then they stopped coming. I had no doubt the wild had swallowed them completely. I was sad that I would most likely never see my two precious little mates again. Our worlds would now no longer meet. But I was also fine with this. I knew we would not be living at this remote outstation for long. They would have kept me anchored to this place if they were still returning to see me and made it hard for me to leave them behind. I was relieved they had become totally independent of us. They had taken their freedom and given me mine.

Experiences like this are the blessings and heartaches of our love and the deep connection we share with our animal friends. Loving and letting go. Allowing and empowering the animals to choose their path even when it soars away from us. How much easier it would sometimes be to not love so deeply, and yet how bereft our lives would be without that holy flame of love that lights us up from deep within.

Adapted from 'Tracks of Love'

Twenty-Nine

Inspirational Lovely

H anging upside down now and squawking with merriment from the branch above our head is a little white corella, that from the first moment she arrived in our lives was so utterly endearing she became known as Lovely.

But, before I share Lovely's story, she wants me to tell you more about the animals on our planet that have consciously chosen to incarnate at this time of massive transformation to be light keepers.

Just like us, many animals are anchoring new realities. Some come to assist their own species, while some come to be guiding lights and help us heal our pain. Others bring awareness and help us see more clearly. Many others, especially our domesticated dogs and cats, provide a channel for unresolved emotions to be expressed, be that sorrow, love or rage!

Many animals walk a hard path because of people's unawakened state, especially our beloved mirror keepers, the wild cats, foxes, dingos and wolves who bravely chose to be the mirror holders so we could see our own out-of-balance reflection.

Nowadays we are seeing more and more farm animals, which we often didn't get an opportunity to know personally, are finding their way out of the meat industry and into sanctuaries and the hearts of people. Every cow and her calf that breaks out of the cycle of suffering and creates a life of love holds that energy for other cows to reclaim their divine right to live in love too. Every pig that breaks out of the confines of its cruel crate and lives to wallow in the mud in peace and sleep under a shady tree is an anchor for other pigs to break free too. Every lamb born in freedom, love and respect is birthing a new energy of kindness and love on our earth and anchoring that reality for others still suffering because the only value put on their lives is financial.

Oh, my loves, together we are changing this. I know it is not easy hearing these truths, but unless we are willing to shine a light into the shadows and illuminate what has been hidden from us, the same old cycle of suffering will continue.

We have been fooled by the illusion of the body and its current form. Many faeries and other elementals, dragons and even people, incarnate into animal or other forms to hold the light as the vibration on our planet shifts from darkness to light.

When we look beyond the physical forms we begin to get an inkling that nothing is as it appears and that our focus on the physical is rather a limiting way to see.

For Lovely, who just like many of us chose to incarnate onto our planet to hold the light, her path wasn't always easy.

For many years, she lived as a wild bird. She had a mate and she reared many nests of young. Then, one day, when she wasn't paying full attention as she swooped down near a road, a car hit her and she suffered a broken wing. That's when life as she knew it came to an end!

She arrived at our sanctuary seven years after this incident. For the first seven years after her accident she had been kept in a small cage. Her broken wing had never received medical attention and sadly it had healed, badly deformed. Can you imagine what it would be like to soar through the sky, dipping and diving, screeching with joy, and all of a sudden your wing is broken and you face the rest of your life earthbound? You will never fly through the sky again. You will never fly with your family and friends again. Everything about your life has shrunk to the size of cage or, if you're lucky, a back yard.

I often go through the emotional struggle a parrot faces when this becomes their reality, and the question always arises, to euthanase or not?

With some birds, it's very clear: they have reached the end of the road in their physical body and they are ready to go. But with Lovely it was different. She was very adamant she was here to stay.

Of course we had no idea that this little parrot that had lost everything we would hold dear would be an inspiration to us all, or that far from being the one needing love, it would be she who gave to us!

We can all makes excuses as to why we can't live our lives to the full, why we can't embrace our dreams, get that new job, leave our angry partners, but the truth is, most of the time the only thing holding us back are our excuses. Lovely never did that. Disabled or not she lived life to the full.

With Lovely, we did what we always do when a new parrot comes to live with us. We give them time to become really familiar with us and all the strange noises from all the different animals in our love-filled, but sometimes rather rowdy, environment. We do this before we open the door to their cage and give them the choice to come out, even if it is only to wander around in our garden or sit under a sprinkler on a hot day. We have trees they can climb up into. And, because we had so many unwanted parrots coming to live with us, let me tell you romance and new relationships amongst them were blooming. (And Gill and I ... please don't ever tell them ... if we can do a little matchmaking behind the scenes ... we do!)

While we had our fingers crossed that Lovely would find herself a new mate amongst those still single, little did we know she would play a vital role healing the lost and wounded parrots that arrived at our sanctuary. She was a beacon of light for them.

She lived her life with such joy, her happiness was infectious and we all fell under her charm. She became our resident clown doctor doing the rounds each day, visiting each parrot that still lived in their cage, restricted by their own fears and their beliefs they were not worthy, and she would spend time with each of them.

Many of these parrots arrived emotionally broken from decades sitting in a cage, totally unloved. Sadly, much of the behaviour people laugh at and see as funny in parrots is the manifestation of a broken spirit. For most of these birds, the only interactions they had ever had were with people who were unconscious of the cruelty they inflicted and treated them as a source of fun. Dance cocky dance, or who's a pretty boy, could never sooth the emotional yearning of these birds that are naturally happy and full of love—if they are left in their own environment or get lots of attention as part of a loving family.

When you have lived in a cage for so long, it takes a lot of encouragement, deep healing and moral support to take a step outside, something we didn't always have time to give individually to the number of parrots needing help. But Lovely did, and that's what she came to us for! Bit by bit she encouraged them, backing off when she sensed the parrots getting fearful of all the changes, even if they were for their own good. Many of these birds had no reason to expect or even hope that their lives would fill with love, or that Lovely was helping them to create a wonderful new life. She was their strong arm of support as they took tiny tentative steps outside their comfort zone, until they felt safe enough to come out by themselves.

Some of the parrots she visited had become angry and aggressive after years of neglect and if she got too close, they would try and bite her. No matter what they attempted to do, it never put her off. She would just keep weaving her magic as she filled their lonely lives with light. Love always opens doors, eventually!

Lovely was a beautiful teacher and reminded us constantly of the energy that surges through our lives when we give. She kept her own energy flowing by giving and sharing and she was the most joyful bird we had ever met. Not every bird adjusts as easily to a flightless life and it takes many of them much longer time to activate their own inner joy, but Lovely nudged them all along, reminding them and us, always, of the fun to be had in life, no matter what!

She would greet every new parrot as she climbed up on to their cage and reassured them that they were safe and loved and that they would be fine. Many parrots that arrived at our sanctuary after 50 years kept in a cage in isolation made their very first physical contact with Lovely.

These were huge heartfelt moments. Seeing a parrot reach out and snuggle up with Lovely after being neglected for decades kept all our hearts wide open, and guess what, that kept all our batteries charged up and overflowing too.

We saw many parrots, that had begun aggressively with Lovely, blossom with her love and allow themselves to be touched for the very first time. It may have taken days, weeks or in some poor cases, months. Lovely was so tenacious and each day she would reach out a little more to them until eventually she would be able to sit up close with them and preen them with her beak. Witnessing this healing was always a deeply moving experience for Gill and me.

And in the moments she wasn't doing her rounds Lovely would be screeching with joy as she did acrobatic somersaults from our washing line. Whatever she was doing and wherever she went she exuded so much hilarity, she made us all laugh!

Many parrots were guided to a more expansive experience of life through Lovely, as were Gill and I. Despite her disability and her losses, she never let it get her down or define her giving and loving spirit.

Now I know that many people like to see endings as happy, and have a set way of experiencing that, but labelling events as good or bad only limits our awareness of what is actually occurring, and distorts the truth.

So, let go people. Throw what you no longer need to the wind and let all limitations be blown away. If it was only up to me, I would perhaps have chosen to end Lovely's tale right here, but it is Lovely herself who urges me on. It is important, she tells me, for freedom is never found weighed down with untruths. We are clearing a new path of awareness and dear Lovely is leading us all out of our comfort zones.

Lovely was with us for about four years and in that time she helped many injured souls break free of the confines of a cage and reclaim the life they were always deserving to live. Most found themselves a mate, which was miraculous and so joyful for us to witness after all their years of being unloved and untouched.

One day Lovely wandered into a different area of our sanctuary. She had never done this before. There was a gradual slope to the ground and wanting to keep her safe I was about to go and shoo her back to the main garden when something extraordinary, no, utterly miraculous, occurred.

She began to run down this slope and as she did she flapped her wings and then before we knew it our little white angel with her badly deformed wing took off flying. Flying! I stood astounded. I had never expected, or even imagined, this could ever happen but there she was flying and shrieking with joy as she soared higher and higher. I had tears rolling down my face as I watched her. Our beautiful Lovely, so full of light, who loved so much, had reclaimed her gift of flight.

Would it be a happy ending if I said she were still at our sanctuary helping parrots to heal? Not for me and not for Lovely, who matters most of all in this. What happened next was her conscious choice and we must respect that.

I sank down to the ground, almost in a pose of prayer, as I watched Lovely climb higher and higher in the clear blue sky. She was so high she was bound to attract the eagles; she was in their realms now. All my fears surfaced. I wanted her to be safe and loved and I wanted her home. Even though I knew that death was not an ending, I felt sick when I saw the eagles. I didn't want Lovely to leave us and I couldn't imagine how all the joy she had awakened would continue after she was gone.

I was shielding my eyes with my hand from the sun as I watched her flit across the sky, like a ray of light, with the predators on her tail. Then I lost sight of them all and I began to imagine the worst.

Oh my Goddess, I felt morose. Some animals and birds fill the air you breathe with their presence. I felt like nothing would be the same without Lovely, for any of us.

She did not return home that day, but I didn't give up hope she was still alive. I called her name for days and walked and walked, looking and searching. Everywhere! It was about a week later when I was sitting sewing that I felt compelled to go for a walk. Magnetically, I was being wound in, and the trail I followed through the bush took me to a pile of white feathers that I knew were the remains of Lovely.

I cried when I saw them but I also felt I had been guided to this moment in time, that Lovely had wanted me to find her feathers. She wanted me to let go, to stop searching for her, but she also wanted me to know she still lived. It is death that is the illusion. Over and over again, the animals show us that the only aspect that dies is the body, just like a snake sheds an old skin. When I was finally able to still myself, I could feel her magical presence and this is when she communicated to me.

She told me she had chosen to incarnate and be of service in this lifetime. In order to help other parrots leave their cages she had to know what being caged felt like. She had chosen to sit for seven years experiencing being imprisoned in a small cage. She had learnt what it was like to live unseen. The few people she did see wanted her to dance for them or do silly things. None of them saw the magnificent being of divinity she truly was and not one person looked her in the eyes and asked from their hearts: how are you, are you okay?

This part of her journey had not been an easy time but it had been essential. She had to experience for herself how crushing it was to sit day after day in a cage, separated from her flock, her family and her mate, and feeling so alone with every day whittling away even more hope. The despair of this time had been almost too much for her to bear.

She told me that she had loved her life when she came to live with us, but her earthly work was complete now. She had finished what she had come to do and all the parrots she had wooed and caressed from their cages, who now lived full and happy lives, were able to hold the energy of healing at our sanctuary for those parrots and birds yet to come. They had learnt from her and the healing cycle would continue.

When she took off flying, so out of the blue, it was because she had transcended the physical limitations of her body. But her wing was still weakened, and it had taken every bit of strength for her to fly so high.

Lovely said: I called to our brothers and sisters, the eagles, Kye. I wanted my last moments to be soaring. I had achieved all I had come for and the eagles gave me a great gift as they opened the doorway for me to return to my true home. The transition was so swift; I was soon soaring in the heavenly realms. I felt so light and free. I had been so ready to leave my damaged body behind.

As I walked home, I finally felt at peace with her passing. I was clutching a handful of feathers that she had said we could use in our sacred tool-making. Her feathers were a gift I treasured, for they carried such a beautiful energy of sacred service, of laughter and joy and ultimately transcendence.

Lovely was a light keeper. She had chosen her path to help her kin and when her earthly work was done she soared free.

From 'Sacred Journey into the Animal Realms'

Thirty

Daisy, Beau & Badger

We always kept an eye on the old bloke who lived just down the dirt track from us. Apart from an ice-addicted daughter, he didn't appear to have any immediate support. He was so cantankerous we could understand why. But he was elderly and frail; we wanted to make sure he was OK. Gill often went down with the first aid kit to tend an untreated wound our elderly neighbour had ignored. He lived in such squalor, any infections were likely to escalate.

Then his ice-addicted ex-military daughter came to stay with him, and she bought her staffy dog that was pregnant. She was hopeful she would make some money selling pups, which concerned us. She was a drama Queen and appeared to go from one disaster to the next. Everything she touched she destroyed, but there was nothing we could do except give her and her dad a wide berth.

Occasionally, we would see our neighbour walking all the pups-all nine of them. He was very frail and walked slowly with the aid of staff while the pups tugged and tussled around him. It was evident he loved those puppies and their morning walks. I got the impression that this daily ritual was an escape from the constant drama and tantrums of his daughter, who appeared to be draining the life force from him. Each time we saw him, he looked worse. While we were concerned about him, we were also aware that weeks were passing, and no attempt was being made to find these puppies' homes.

So I offered to take some beautiful photos of them playing in nature for his daughter, who told us she would sell them online. Despite doing this, she made endless excuses why they couldn't be rehomed. *People weren't willing to pay; she didn't trust that person; those two pups were a rare colour, and she should keep them for herself.*

Nothing we did to try and help made any difference. They had nine three-month-old puppies, and I knew if they didn't act soon, we would likely witness more breeding disasters as brothers and sisters mated.

It was the biggest mess. We had done everything we could. We handed the whole situation over to the power of LOVE and let go.

Unexpectedly, help came; a local farmer complained about the pups chasing his sheep, and our neighbour and his daughter were forced to act. They now had to find homes for the puppies. Evidently, the market for trading in staffy dogs was saturated, so I worked with the daughter to send seven pups to a wonderful animal rescue. She adamantly refused to part with two dogs, and she became so volatile when I tried to persuade her, I could only accept. We had rehomed seven. That was progress.

We kept an eye on our neighbour from a distance. Occasionally, we would bump into him, and he was always in a bad state. He was living with a daughter who was draining his energy with her anger towards him. He had never been there as a father. He'd never told her he loved her; she felt let down. While he was completely unable to express or show any feelings, I sensed he wanted to make up for not being there for her as a father. That's why he put up with all her pain.

They lived in a quagmire of unhealed trauma that was eating them both alive. When the daughter finally left, the old bloke started to look a little more like himself, but now he had two grown staffy dogs, and neither had been desexed.

Once again, we offered to help rehome them, but he was adamant they were fine- his daughter may return for them. She would be furious if they were gone. It's very frustrating when you come across these situations. You can see them heading to disaster, but there is nothing you can do but be patient. I have learned, though, that opportunities to help often do eventually come. Sometimes it's all about timing.

To try and avoid these dogs mating, our neighbour fenced off two squalid pens; we have to remember he was living in squalor himself; no one can give to another what they do not give to themselves. These dogs lived as he did, and this is where they stayed for the next year. They no longer went for daily walks or got cleaned out; this guy didn't even have running water; cleanliness was the last priority, *but* they were fed.

Gill often went down to tend to the old man. I found his space too emotionally gruelling and would get upset over the dogs, but Gill could stay in his centre and help wherever possible. On every visit, he cuddled the dogs and reassured them they were loved and had not been forgotten, but they both looked pretty sad. Their lives had become pretty dismal. Periodically, Gill would again broach the subject of rehoming the dogs, but our neighbour was always adamant this was not an option. Despite his protestations, we still held the vision of both dogs finding beautiful, loving homes.

Then, one morning, Gill discovered the female dog had given birth to nine pups. Their squalid pens had evidently failed to prevent any further pups. The whole situation was a mess. Not only were they all living in filth, but six of the nine pups were already dead, and the rest were crawling with ants. Gill was no longer prepared to negotiate with this stubborn old man over the welfare of his dogs. Prior to this incident, no animal welfare organisation would have interfered; if the animal is fed, that's enough for them. We lived in an area where many dogs spent their lives on chains or in pens; most people around us would not have had any concern for these dogs' welfare. Only now, pups had died, and the welfare of the others hung in the balance. Finally, our neighbour agreed that Gill could take the mum and the live pups.

We both felt he was deeply relieved to have them gone.

That is how our dear Daisy landed unexpectedly in our lives with her newborn pups. We had always imagined her having a wonderful new home but never considered it would be with us. We already had a big crew of previously rescued dogs, but Daisy needed help, and we were willing to stretch to help her in her time of need. But despite doing everything we could, only one pup survived. The rest had been hanging by a thread to life when we got them, and they passed away within hours.

I often felt that the life force of those eight pups who'd passed, had been funnelled into the only one that survived. In a beautiful way, though. As if they'd known they hadn't the strength to make it so, they gave it to the one that stood the best chance, and that little pup was so special.

From the moment we saw her, we called her Badger because she had such similar markings. It soon became apparent that Daisy had no milk and did not want to be with her pup. We'd try to coax her into the haven we had created for them, but she was so disconnected from her baby that she kept trying to escape and was very stressed with her puppy.

Left with no option, we began to hand-rear Badger ourselves. Daisy was barely a year old and had given birth in such turmoil it was easy to understand her lack of motherly connection. She was much happier when we let her sleep by the fire on a big, fluffy dog bed. She looked like a Queen.

So Badger became our much-adored wee bub. She had a zest for life that was unstoppable. And a wildness that reminded me of a willy-willy spiralling across the desert, a tumble of autumn leaves falling in a golden-hued cascade of brilliance as the wind picked up. She was a gale-force wind, a hurricane, but she was also a calm and tranquil lake and a night sky glittered with stars. She was everything and thrived despite so many obstacles- she had nearly been eaten alive by ants, we didn't have the right puppy formula, and her mum had rolled on her and squashed her several times.

And while she grew, Badger always remained this tiny little blue staffy.

We had ten dogs by this time; Daisy had settled into their midst. We live very remote, and I was not keen to send her on an animal transporter to be rehomed. I felt she had been through enough. She loved being with us, her new comforts, regular walks, and a bed to sleep on - all perfectly normal things for any happy dog, yet this little love had been denied them. I loved witnessing her bloom. She also made friends with Badger, and they would often share a bed or go down the river together; it was beautiful to see their newfound connection.

But we had not forgotten the remaining dog. He was living in an utter hovel. We did our best to keep it clean, but there was no water there, and while a clean space was important, it wasn't his biggest struggle. Staffys are super affectionate people dogs; they thrive on human connection. To spend so long sitting alone and untouched was denying this dog his basic nature. One day, I cupped his face gently in my hands, looked him in the eyes, and promised him I would find him the most fantastic home.

Then, a miracle happened. It's often the way with these stubborn animal owners that the significant shift for their animals happen when they get sick. Our neighbour had to go to hospital and *finally* agreed we could rehome the remaining dog.

Hallelujah.

I would have loved to gather him up and bring him straight home to our place, but I couldn't. He had not been desexed; we were already working with a new big male dog we had taken on, and we didn't want to risk Daisy getting pregnant again. She was booked to be desexed, but the deed had not yet been done.

But I was a woman on a mission. I asked the Universe to guide me to find the perfect home for Smooches. He had never had a name before then.

Within a few hours, I had organised for him to go to the Staffy rescue in Melbourne; they were confident, with his colouring, they would find him a perfect home. I was hesitant to send him so far, but every cell in my body tingled with light. I knew this was his path; this way, he would find the people who would deeply love him and give him everything he deserved. Miraculously, the animal transport to Melbourne was passing through a town one hundred kilometres away the following day. We organised to meet them.

I confess I shed many tears when I put him on that truck. He was such a stoic and patient dog with a still energy that was very Buddha-like. He had been through so much I did not want him to suffer in any way ever again. *TRUST* a voice said to me from within, *it will all work out perfectly,* and it did. It worked out even better than I could have imagined and I still cry tears of joy that this noble dog found two people that utterly adore him.

Apparently, the rescue had over a hundred applicants for him, and they sifted through them very carefully and only felt that one application was the perfect match.

His new guardians called him Beau, and every birthday; I get pictures of Beau sitting at a table with his own birthday cake. He could not be more loved. He goes for long walks on the beach and is the focus of their attention.

As for Daisy, she is still in our tribe. Six years later, living the good life. Enjoying walks and all the joys of being loved, but little Badger, well, I call her our shooting star.

Let me tell you about her.

She lived with us for three years, and it was glaringly obvious, even if I ached to deny it, that she lived in a blaze of such intensity and light that I knew her earthly passage would be swift. I have had other animals like this. They are remarkable; they are different from the others. While the rest of our dogs would dive under cover in a storm, Badger would be out in the open paddock, dancing and frolicking as lightning struck around her. I had never seen anything like it. This dog was ignited by the energy of a storm and thrived on the power of lightning. She was a fearless and mighty force of nature who was always off on some adventure, even by herself. Chasing leaves, scrambling at the water's edge as she tried to grab reflections, chasing her tail- many thought we should stop her, but I always felt it was her way of anchoring the excessive electrical currents that surged through her. She was doing what she needed to stabilise. Outside, she was a phenomenon, but indoors, she was serene, sweet, and calm. I more than adored her, but I knew when she was a tiny pup, she could not live a long life at the intensity she did. She had only come to blaze through our lives as a force of light - just like a shooting star.

Oh yes, I wanted to hang on to her, keep her safe, prevent her from leaving. She was a gift in so many ways, but in the end, she passed swiftly and unexpectedly from a cause even the vet could not identify. One minute, she was dancing wildly with the storm; the next, she was gone.

Our lovely little Badger

And I tell this story because we succeeded in our vision with Daisy and Beau. After all, we never gave up. We kept holding love and seeing the outcome, and while it took some time to manifest, it happened and was even better than I imagined.

Badger, well, she was the blessing of those times; she was the holy gift that lit up our lives and showed us how powerful we are when we live fearlessly, and I will always be grateful for that.

Thirty-One

Jess Loves Life

We live very remote, right in the midst of cotton and wheat farms and sheep and cattle stations. The locals shake their heads in puzzlement when they see our animals. Why would a sane person have so many animals and not profit from them? It's not something we can even explain- compassion is not a language that is understood here. We do what we do here because we know it makes a difference. Every sheep that gets to live a full and happy life of love holds that frequency for their kin to experience similar. Every dog that breaks free from a life on a chain holds space for other dogs to experience expansion too.

But it can be challenging living where we do. Animal welfare is not a concern, and we often deal with situations that challenge us to stay calm, be patient and play our hand like a grand master chess player. If we barged in, guns firing, every door would close to us, and we would not be able to help the animals we do.

Unfortunately, this was the case with Jess. As hard as it was to be patient, we just had to bide our time.

Like many dogs around here, she lived in a hovel of a tiny pen with no blanket or warm bed. When she was periodically let out, she looked manic. She reminded me of patients I'd met in mental institutions many years ago when I used to work in that field. I had watched her several times and wondered whether the emotional damage Jess had experienced could be healed. I believed it could, but in all my years of helping animals, I had not met an animal that felt as disconnected from her physical body as she did. It was as if she'd checked out ages ago, and her body was only a vacant shell.

For a year, we hovered on the edges of her life, holding the vision of the perfect opportunity to help her. There were many days I despaired an opportunity would ever come.

Then I had a beautiful dream. I was told to prepare for the arrival of Jess, that she was coming and her healing would be my healing. The trauma she had to release was deeply connected with my own feelings of being unseen, unheard and unloved.

I have had these powerful dreams many times before, and while I felt it was prophetic, I didn't even want to hold hope. I had been waiting for this dear old girl for so long, but I didn't have to wait much longer. Within a couple of days, her elderly owner came to see us. He was going to the hospital and would be away for several weeks. He was concerned about Jess because there was no one to care for her. He didn't ask us if we could help him; he told us she was going to be shot!

The words came tumbling out of my mouth, 'Noooooooo, don't do that! If you are going to shoot her, we will take her on.'

Our moment had arrived and within a few hours, Jess was delivered to us.

She was cowering and cringing when she came. She froze if I reached out to touch her. I knew we would have to take little steps to gain her trust. We put her in a dog crate inside our home. At one end, I had made her a comfy bed, but she sat on the floor beside it. She was very suspicious of her bed; it took days before she moved on to it. It was such a wondrous moment when she finally did, and she looked at us with a hint of a smile. It was her first comfy and warm bed- ever!

Vacating her body had been her way of coping with the scarcity of love in her life, but it didn't take her long to return. She soon adjusted to the lead and was easy to take for a walk, but she was still very nervous about being touched. I spent a lot of time with her, gently talking to her and reaching out so she could sniff my hand. I wanted her to know that we would listen to her. We would not violate her boundaries. If she was uncomfortable being touched, we would not touch her.

Oh, it was hard. I ached to cuddle this girl but knew that gift would come.

As the weeks passed, she began to open up much more. She let me rub her nose, and when she walked past me, she brushed her body against my legs. We had reached the stage of opening the crate door. She was responsive, would come when called, and thoroughly enjoyed her new life. This dog had the biggest smile. She was smiling in every photo I took of her sitting beside me. When an animal that has been broken trusts you enough to give you their love, well, that to me is the treasure of these often hard earnt experiences.

I had often pondered the message in the dream that had foretold Jess's arrival. I had often experienced my own liberation from illusory limitations when helping an animal overcome theirs. But I could feel that Jess and I were similar. I, too, had left my body to cope with trauma. I had also felt very unheard and unseen in my past. Many people in my life had treated me as if I didn't matter or even had a right to say no or make a different choice. I'd often struggled with feelings of powerlessness, but a situation occurred that forced me to stand in my power and be heard.

The elderly man who had brought us Jess turned up to collect her. It had not even occurred to me that this could happen. After all, his plan was to shoot her! He had been away for several months, and now he wanted her back.

A part of me was shaking. Did he have the right? Should I have got him to sign her over? Most likely, yes, but it hadn't occurred to me then. I thought we had a straight-forward arrangement. I had no idea there would be any confusion. I reared up like a cobra about to strike. There was no way I would return Jess to the dismal life she'd had. I stood my ground and refused to hand her over. I also made it very clear that he was going to shoot her. She would be dead if her care had been left to him. He'd even told us to shoot her if she became too much. *Yeah, as if that was likely to happen!*

And this man was not cruel. You would most likely love him if you met him, but he was an old farmer and in-grained in his ways. Dogs had their place- outside. There was no questioning the emotional welfare of keeping them on a chain or in a small cage. When people can't nourish their emotional needs, they cannot do it for animals.

He may not have realised the truth in my words if I had not spoken with passion and fury. But he got it and backed off. He agreed that Jess was in a better situation with us.

I had stood in disbelief when he turned up and asked for his dog back. My whole body trembled because I didn't know if he had that right. Morally, ethically, certainly not, but legally? I didn't know. I had guided Jess back into life and love, and the prospect of betraying her trust was sickening. I literally wanted to spew.

The relief I felt when he left was so overwhelming I fell to my knees crying. Jess had run and hid when she saw her old owner turn up, and I found her cowering in the corner of my bus, hoping that no one would see her.

'It's ok', I whispered as I coaxed her out; 'he has gone now, and your home is with us". She came out so eagerly, wagging her tail. We walked along the river bank. I needed to de-stress and reconnect with nature. It was a beautiful day; spoonbills were wading in the shallows, and the sky was a clear, bright blue; light sparkles danced on the surface of the river. Everything felt tranquil. My peace of mind was restored, and then Jess started barking. I had not heard her bark before. She had been so shut down and existed as if she had no right to take up any space. I laughed. The day had forced me to be heard, and now Jess was having her say. I called her to me, but she was still barking excitedly at the base of an old gum tree that grew on the water's edge. It had huge flowing branches and such grace and beauty I had named this tree Dancer. There, perched high up on a silvery limp of the tree, were two huge wedge-tailed eagles, and they were looking down at us—me and my mate Jess, healing old patterns together. I knew our day had been momentous in breakthroughs, and the wise and powerful eagles acknowledged this. It was so rare to see them; there were far fewer of them than previously, but somehow, these two had found their way to us.

But let me tell you more about the elderly man because his story doesn't end here. He had two other dogs, while they still lived a rough old life; they had been working dogs and had a much closer bond with him than Jess ever had. They had also spent a lot of time working sheep, which had given them a reprieve from the emotional toll of a life caged. It had been easier for him to find people to look after them; they did not have the issues Jess did. However, their life began to change for the better when this man, our neighbour, began to witness the shifts happening for Jess.

Some people have such big lights in some aspects of their lives and such density in others. Perhaps we are all a little like this. Our neighbour grew vegetables for our small community and would box them up and deliver them for free, so he often called in. As Jess made more progress, she became more confident about coming out. He would deliver his spinach and cauliflower and see Jess all rugged up in a fleecy dog jacket. The next time we saw his dogs, they were wearing dog jackets, too! Then he bought them beds and blankets. Little changes that made a massive difference to the welfare of those dogs in winter. The love and care we gave our animals had rubbed off on an old farmer who had never experienced animals being treated with compassion before.

Love is contagious; plant seeds of LOVE everywhere, especially in dark places where it has never ever been sewn before.

Thirty-Two

Love expands us

M any decades ago, I was at a healing group and mentioned to one of the women that I was look-ing for somewhere to live. She knew I had a couple of dogs and immediately replied, 'Oh, you'll never get somewhere nice to live with dogs'.

I thought about this for a while and concluded that it made absolutely no sense. In a magical and wondrous universe, to be always destined to have less than the best because I loved animals seemed to me to be utterly insane! Even more amazing and wonderful things should happen *because* I loved dogs. It didn't take me long to remove this woman's limiting statement; it had no rele-vance in my life.

Within a week I had scored the most magnificent home to rent. It was a beautiful old Queenslander on a seven-ty-acre peninsular that overlooked the Coral Sea from three sides of the house! It was nestled into a circle of ancient frangipani trees and peeped out from magenta bougainvillea with a bush lemon tree I could pick fruit from, straight from the sunroom window! It was paradise.

I had my own private tracks to two different tropical beaches, and understandably, I felt like I was in heaven. I couldn't help smiling when the woman who'd told me I wouldn't get anywhere nice to live asked me how I had manifested such a fantastic home. I told her it was because I loved dogs and the Universe looked after me!

But there is even more wondrousness to share in this tale.

I had taken a huge leap of faith with the rent. It was an enormous expense on my meagre income, but I wanted to live in this beautiful house so much I didn't hesitate. Somehow, I would make this work.

Within a few weeks, my landlady had put the rent down because she said the house was messy when we moved in. A month after that, she knocked even more off the weekly rent. While my friends' rents were all soaring, mine continued to decline until about eight months later, I was living in my paradise home, totally rent-free, and I enjoyed this benefit for many wonderful years.

Now, there is a huge reason the animals want me to share this experience. So many people limit their experiences of manifesting a perfect home by making fearful statements like the woman I met did. Many people who deeply love their dog will part with them because they can't take them to their new home.

The animal kingdom wants to tell you that when parting with your dog is not an option, the rentals that won't accept dogs no longer come into your sphere. Your world expands because of your love for an animal; it is only your fearful thoughts that contract the abundance of your possibilities. If you love your dog, keep it. It is limiting thought that needs to go, not your beloved dog!

However, I have discovered in my own life that my refusal to part with the animals I love has often led me on unexpected magical adventures. If my chosen route demands that I contract my energy and shave from my life what I love, it is not a path worth walking. That, for me, is a clear sign I am walking in the wrong direction. Our animals are our sacred guides. When we reject options that demand we rehome our dog, other options appear, although they may look very different from the stability and routine of the familiar. We may need to take a leap of faith and trust in how our life is unfolding.

I recall another time when Gill and I were looking for a home, and despite doing everything we could to get one, nothing local manifested. The only door that was open was the opportunity to rent a bush home on some acreage several hundred kilometres away. A friend had come across it and told me she thought it was our dream home, but I resisted this new direction. We had five dogs, and we were sleeping on the beach at night or camping with friends. I felt desperate for a home but didn't want to move or leave people who were dear to me behind.

In the end, we were left with no other choice but to trust in the only option we had - the bush home on acreage, a place we knew loved and welcomed our dogs.

It was a five-hour journey away, and our soft-top Nissan G60 was laden with all our belongings and our five much-loved dogs. I was exhausted by the time we arrived but horrified by the home we had hoped would be our haven. A massive sign greeted us in red dripping paint: TRESPASSERS WILL BE SHOT. When we went to get the key from the neighbour, she told us to keep an eye on our dogs; if they got out, the farmer would shoot them. When we opened the door to the house that was situated on a very bleak and depressing bush block, the inside was awful. Every cupboard was full of clothes, beds were all made up, and fridges were full of food. There was no room in this home for us to make a life, even if we wanted to, which we didn't!

After returning the key to the neighbour, we sat in the car pondering what to do. We had just exhausted our only option. I was in tears when Gill said, 'Let's go to Broome'. For a moment, I thought he had gone utterly mad. Broome was four thousand kilometres away; we had barely any money. The retreads on the car were already peeling; it sounded like a ludicrous idea, or was it?

At that moment, the clouds parted, and what had been a dismal day was bathed in the most beautiful light. It was a sign from the Universe, we were going to Broome. This horrible little property had only served to lure us away from the safe and familiar and open us up to wilder and more magical possibilities. It had been a stepping stone on our treasure trail of life.

Five days later, after driving over four thousand kilometres, we had only fifty dollars left when we finally arrived in Broome. The retreads had got us across those harsh desert miles, but they looked shabby. We were living totally on the edge.

I certainly had some fears about how we would manage to buy food and feed our dogs, let alone find somewhere lovely to live. I knew I had to stay positive, so I let go of my fears and imagined the best.

Within a few days, we had scored a fabulous home on the beach, and when I asked the landlord if he minded dogs, he said no, he loved them. 'Five?' I asked nervously. 'Absolutely no problem', he replied. I held my breath as I told him about our dire financial situation. That was okay, he said; we could begin paying in a few weeks when the new month started.

We were even supported in our abundance by some new friends, who lent us some money to get our clothing business up and running, which we easily repaid in a few weeks. And we did all this *with* our big family of dogs.

I have travelled all around Australia with dogs. I have journeyed in a camel wagon with over fifty rescued animals in tow, and no matter how big my family, people have still invited us back to stay and offered us beautiful places to live.

We need to trust more in our magical lives because the consequences of not trusting go way beyond us and impact so many animals that end up unwanted and unloved because people didn't realise how powerful they were, and they gave up on their friends.

Our paths are magical treasure trails that unfold and bloom like a rose unfurls from being a bud, but only when our choice is LOVE.

Love always, LOVE.

Thirty-Three

Holy Cats

G ill and I had never previously had a cat. We had almost every other type of animal- pigs, camels, goats, parrots, sheep, horses, dogs, chickens, doves, emus, just not cats.

Then, one morning, we drove to town, which was an hour away, and I had the strongest knowing we had to check the two cages, just outside our local tip where people left unwanted animals. I was not too fond of the idea that people could leave animals in a cage, but it was better than dumping them out in the bush.

As we pulled alongside them, I noticed both doors were open. There were obviously no animals inside; even so, I decided to go and look. Sitting on the concrete floor in one of the cages was a young black and white cat, about four months old, and he was crying. In a pile beside him were various toys, including a pink crocheted mouse, a fluffy ball with a bell, and a small crocheted blanket.

It was heartbreaking to witness this cat's distress at his change in circumstances. He was making the most pitiful sound. I gathered him into my arms and cuddled him. He was shaking all over. Gill reassured me that the ranger would come and pick him up, but I wasn't prepared to leave a crying cat. I could sense Gill was aloof because it was a cat. It wasn't that he didn't like them; he just, understandably, worried about the birds.

'Look, Gill, we are not going to keep him, but if we can organise to meet the ranger or drop him off somewhere he will be looked after, that's all I want'. When I asked Gill to hold the cat while I called the ranger, he pulled away. He was worried that the magnetic pull of this dumped feline would sway him into cat ownership. 'If I hold him, he is coming home, I know it'

'Gill, I can't phone the ranger and hold the cat', I replied as I placed the puss in his arms and dialled for help. There was no reply from the ranger, so I left a message. 'OK, we will put the cat in the car and wait for her return call', I told Gill firmly. He was behaving like a baby over this cat.

We sat in the car waiting, and there was no return call. We tried to ring again, but there was no answer. We left the cat sleeping happily in our car, went for a coffee, and asked everyone in the cafe if they wanted a cat. No luck. We returned to our sleeping puss and decided to go about our day, and as soon as we heard from the ranger, we would drop the cat off. We didn't get any returned calls, but Gill did receive a holy message. 'His name is Dimple', he just told me!

'What do you mean he just told you his name?' I asked, looking deeply puzzled, 'Why would he tell you his name when we are about to hand him over to the ranger?'

'Because he is coming home with us', Gill replied. He had been right; one cat cuddle, and they had claimed him.

And that is how our noble and most dignified Mr Dimple came into our lives, but he was not the end of this cat contagion- there were more!

One night, Gill had a very vivid dream about the wild cats that sometimes predated on our birds. We had tried to figure out a solution; we didn't want to encourage them by feeding them, and we certainly didn't want to kill them, though there has been an occasion when Gill had to put down a predator that was marauding and killing our animals, but that was always the last resort.

In Gill's dream, he is shown two cats with no tails, like a Lynx, and told that they are coming and we must not harm them because they are holy temple cats. We were unsure which cats these were, but we were about to find out.

Within a few days, I found a young cat, about three months old, in an aviary that housed an injured crow.

The kitten was mantling over a piece of meat the crow had dropped. As I got close, it began to spit and hiss ferociously. I called Gill, and together, we caught the kitten and put it in a large cage in the midst of our home so we could domesticate it and get it desexed. It would be a huge win if we could stop these cats from breeding.

I had seen this young cat before. In fact, I had witnessed Mr Dimple humping it. So I presumed it was a female cat, and as it was still quite young, I was hopeful it had not got pregnant. But the cat contagion did not end there. Within a couple of days, a hissing sound came from the corner of our kitchen. It startled all our dogs, and they began barking. When we looked behind the cupboard, we found another young cat. How it had entered our home without being detected by our six always-on-the-alert dogs was, frankly, miraculous. It looked as if it had come from the same tabby litter as the one we had just caught. Mr Dimple ran over to welcome it, and I realised this puss was also one of his mates. Mr Dimple had not only swayed a man determined never to own a cat into willing and eager feline obedience, but he was also apparently inviting his friends. Within a few weeks, we had gone from no cats to three cats.

But of course, our latest two tabby cats, spitting and hissing with feral fury, had been prophesied in a dream. What can one do in the face of such divine momentum but go with the flow?

The two wilduns quickly adapted to domesticity and were soon purring in contentment. When they were finally tame enough for a trip to the vet, we discovered they were not girls; they were both boys.

And the birds, well, our friendly magpie, gave them hell. It truly put them in their place. We'd hand-reared it from a tiny chick when it had been blown from its nest in a wild storm. It lived its life wild and free yet always returned home. All the dogs were used to its crazy antics, and the cats had to learn too. None of our three pussy's would dare eat their food when Tutti, our magpie, was around for fear of being swiped by its ferocious beak.

Magpies are so clear on boundaries, and our three little felines learnt very fast.

And that is how Mr Dimps, and our Holy cats, Pie-pie and Furphy came into our lives, serendipitously, guided, and prophesied.

And now we are their willing slaves.

Please leave a Review

I am a self published author and all profits from this book help us to continue to care for not only ourselves, but an already large family of previously rescued animals. The more books we sell, the more we can do to help even more animals and build our vision of kindness. If you have enjoyed this book please let your friends know. Share it on social media. Gift it to your friends.

We thank you. We appreciate you. So much LOVE

Kye & Gill & all the animals.

Ps . If you would like to join our mailing list for periodic love letters

www.kyecrow.love

And if you have your own awesome animal experience you would like to submit for consideration for future books, please contact Kye via the website.

Love We Live

How innocently I made that phone call. Completely unaware that the consequences of that day would shift the direction of my life forever, and that what was about to enter my life would lead me so far away from my comfort zones, I would never walk the well-worn paths again.

I had tossed and turned all through the night after our conversation. Dreaming up one excuse after another to bail out, but deep down I knew I wouldn't use any of them. I had offered to help and I felt honour bound to go.

Now there were several reasons I was not looking forward to the day. In truth, even though I had made a friendly offer to help someone who'd just split up from her partner, I barely knew Adi. I liked her, was curious about her, but often found her very distant to be around. The prospect of spending an entire day with her felt a little daunting.

But there was a much more pressing reason and one I had not anticipated when I made my innocent offer. You see I had imagined baby-sitting her daughter, helping her move some boxes of stuff, even cooking her a dinner after a long day - but instead she had roped me into moving two camels, twenty kilometres. She had leapt on my offer of help with such unexpected eagerness for someone usually so restrained, I couldn't find any way to back out. I knew I wouldn't be any help to her. I had only met a camel once before and he had been drooling copious amount of saliva and had lunged at me with such aggression, I had no desire to *ever* meet one again.

Yes, I felt scared! I wanted to run away as fast as I could but the day had an inevitability about it that was stronger than me. It was happening whether I liked it or not.

Adi arrived just after dawn with a friend I'd not met before and I wasn't immediately enamoured. On first meeting he seemed a bit full of himself. In his early forties, wearing high heeled cowboy boots and perfecting a cocky strut, Adi introduced me to Eagle. While his overall attire was cowboy, black shirt tucked into neat and tidy jeans, there was also an aspect of hippy. Hanging around his neck was a large quartz crystal amulet and his black Akubra hat was adorned with feathers.

In his hand he carried a jumbo pack of cigarettes, prepared and ready to chain smoke anywhere. I had no idea then that by the end of the day I would be shaking like a leaf and sucking on Winnie blues with him.

He was loud and boisterous and slapped me on the back as if I was a long lost friend and as the three of us piled into Adi's car, I couldn't help noticing - Eagle was the only one enjoying himself.

For twenty kilometres we drove down a bumpy corru-gated red dirt road, through a landscape of giant tumble-weeds and salt bush, laced with patches of wildflowers. The desert had grown lush from all the recent rains and I couldn't help feeling deeply moved by the splendour of the bush, the terracotta coloured road and the flocks of white corellas that would swoop across the bright blue sky, twisting and turning and swirling in the light.

By the time we pulled into the paddock where Adi's camels were, I had softened to the experience. I had let go of the fight, I was even warming to Eagle who wasn't as brash or full of himself as my first impressions had led me to believe. He was actually really likeable and had a rare childlike quality about him that led him to embrace life with excitement and even though he was a horse man with no experience of camels, he was pretty confident his equine skills would come in handy.

While Adi tooted the horn of her car to call the camels in, Eagle and I walked out to a small red sandhill, hoping to get high enough to see the camels coming in from a distance. The paddock was so big, you could walk for a day and not hit a fence - but the camels were familiar with the car horn and Adi was certain they would come.

Twenty minutes passed of horn tooting and searching for humps and finally we saw them weaving their way through the mulga and witchetty bush, to us. They walked in a haze, with the dust billowing around them and from my distance, the harsh desert light made them look as if they'd been bleached. All my fears were forgotten and I felt a flush of excitement. We sat for a while, watching as they approached and as they got closer Eagle and I began walking towards them, eager to meet them. Adi had reassured us they were all friendly.

I was standing innocently out on the flat as the first camel came towards me. He was so much bigger than I'd anticipated from a distance and he barged straight up to me, totally ignoring my outstretched hand. He had absolutely zero respect for my space and I found this frightening. He stood towering above me menacingly, with his body almost pressed up against mine and his drooling mouth smeared right up against my face.

I had not expected this and although I was doing my best not to panic, inside I was freaking out.

Deep breath Kye, don't panic, best not to run, deep breath, that's it my girl you're doing fine, just keep breathing and stay calm.

It was so hard. I was struggling not to panic and at the same time trying to look casually around me for a safe place to reach, but the car or the nearest tree was too far away and Adi seemed completely oblivious to my situation. There was nowhere close enough for me to go, and the camel was getting more and more menacing, jumping around me and kicking out its legs. I couldn't even see a stick on the ground I could use to defend myself.

I felt so intimidated, my mouth was dry with fear. I had no idea what to do, I only knew it was wise to stay calm. If I ran his game would be on. It was in that moment of desperate realisation that I had nowhere safe to go that I saw Eagle and it's a moment I shall never forget.

He was ambling towards me, totally absorbed in his thoughts. His well-worn black Akubra hat giving some shade from the sun, his face a picture of contentment, he looked as if he was in the midst of recalling happy memories. The time he had tamed the wild stallion, or lassoed the runaway cow, or swung through the trees like Tarzan. We had heard many tales of Eagle's daring feats on the drive down and as I watched him approach, I felt myself sigh. Eagle would know what to do. Eagle would help. Relief flooded through me.

There is something that happens when you're drenched with fear. Everything appears to slow down and there is a sharpening of senses. Every detail is noticed, every heart beat heard. I saw the exact moment that Eagle became present to his surroundings. I watched the contented smile slip away from his face. I saw him stop dead in his tracks as danger hit him in the guts. I felt the very moment my intimidator took all his attention from me and focused it on Eagle with such a ferocious intensity, he was almost licking his lips in anticipatory pleasure as he watched this lone cowboy approach. There was a brief moment when Eagle and the camel locked eyes and then Eagle, with no pretence of bravery, turned and took off running for his life, his high heeled cowboy boots kicking up the dust leaving hard edged tracks in the desert sand as the red maniac of a camel galloped after him.

I was so shaken by the experience I collapsed on the ground laughing hysterically. I had tears rolling down my face. I felt sick and wanted to have a shit all at the same time and I only began breathing again when I saw Eagle make it to safety!

Eagle and I from that moment on were united in our fear of camels. We clung to each other, initiated into our camel terror together. Forever brother and sister, bonded eternally by the day we had almost been trampled by the rogue red camel from hell. Neither of us were any help to Adi, who made no attempt to even conceal her scorn for us.

It had taken hours in the hot sun to catch one young camel because Adi was doing it single-handed. Every time the camel ran towards Eagle or me we would run as if we were being chased and hide, petrified in the trees.

Finally Adi, with the skill of a well-seasoned cowgirl which she wasn't, lassoed and caught the young camel she wanted to take. Kunkaa was only six months old and her mother was in such poor condition she looked like a walking skeleton. Separating Kunkaa from her mother was a hard choice for anyone to make, but If Adi didn't take the baby, mum would surely die.

I felt so relieved when the three camels were finally tethered from the back of Adi's small sedan car and we set off on the slow and bumpy drive home. It was getting late in the day and there was no doubt we would be driving well into the dark.

Adi's expectations of the jobs she thought I would be suitable for constantly kept falling outside of my 'can do' zone. Arming me with a huge block of wood, she wanted me to hang out the front passenger window and bash the big red camel who had terrorised me and Eagle with a block of wood in an attempt to stop him eating the car!

We had learned his name was Abdul and he was straining on his rope to get the rear vision mirror in his mouth. I gave him a wee whack, nothing happened. It made zero impact and did not deter him from his focus on the destruction of the mirror.

"Hit him harder," Adi said impatiently. Even though this camel had put me through hell, hitting him was not something I could do. We swapped places in a stony silence and I drove, at five kilometres an hour. I faced hours of driving in the heat with sweat pouring down my face and almost zero conversation with Adi, but at least driving was something I *could* do.

Way off in the distance, just a pinprick on the horizon, was Eagle. Despite the searing heat of the sun he had refused to ride in the car and had vowed never to go near a camel again, ever. Nothing we said would convince him to come anywhere near the car. He knew the camels were on short ropes, but he wasn't taking *any* chances.

He hobbled the twenty kilometres back in his high heeled cowboy boots, blistering his swollen feet and I would have joined him if I could have. I would have hobbled down that rough desert road and blistered my feet with him. It was cloying in the car. Adi does not suffer fools and is often so remote, and the silence that had settled between us was suffocating.

I was so relieved as we got closer to town to see Gill driving out to meet us. As the light had faded he had decided to come and see if we were all ok. My biggest concern was Eagle who had fallen so far behind, we had not seen him for a few hours. Gill drove back and found him, staggering along in the dark, badly dehydrated and bright red from sun burn.

The two male camels we'd towed behind had been revolting creatures. The other male camel was in season and bubbling froth and spittle all over the place. The only redemption for their species was little Kunkaa who despite leaving her mother behind, had walked the twenty kilometres stoic and uncomplaining. Regardless of the grace of this chocolate brown calf, I, just like Eagle, never wanted to see another camel EVER, EVER again.

It wasn't until a week later that I found out something that Adi had failed to tell us, or perhaps it was something she had failed to admit to herself, but Eagle and I were not the only ones who had been predated on by Abdul. While he behaved like an angel for Adi and her ten year old daughter, the list of people he had terrorised was lengthy and included experienced cameleers who had climbed trees to escape him, and police officers who had been chased around their squad car and eventually had to stay on the roof until help came. I even heard of one woman who had spent hours running between her car and her gate that she was trying to open so she could drive out to work. She didn't make it to work that day.

While it was a miracle no-one had ever been hurt, it was even more miraculous that Abdul, in his reign of terror, had not been shot.

Naughty Abdul had originally come from the small out-back town of Oodnadatta, hand reared and allowed to grow up without clear boundaries. Drinking beer in the pub, he was generally seen as source of amusement until the cute antics of a baby camel became dangerous the bigger he got. It's pretty sad to imagine the confusion he must have felt when he got driven out of town but Abduls story is not unique. Numerous tales exist of people who have hand reared orphan camels, brought them up without any boundaries or discipline, allowing them to come into the house, laughing at all sorts of dysfunctional behaviour and then shooting them when they become too dangerous to be around.

But Abdul was one of the lucky ones and was rescued by Adi from his lone life on the local rubbish tip when she trekked through Oodnadatta with her own camels. She obviously adored him, but after the day I'd had with him, I had yet to understand why and I was certain I never would.

I was so relieved when I said goodbye to Adi and her camels. It had taken us fifteen hellish hours since leaving early that morning. I was dirty and tired and had not eaten all day. I just wanted to get home.

Eagle and I clung to each other as we said goodbye, tears rolling down our faces and promised to stay in touch, both still shaking from the traumas of the day, both adamant our camel days were done. I had told Gill as we drove home, "I am definitely NOT a camel woman Gill." I was so clear about that.

It had been a long time since I'd dreamt of Gill walking towards me leading three humped beasts and it would be another year before, like sunshine streaming through the clouds, that I'd finally make that connection. Camels were coming into my life whether I liked it OR NOT! And they had already begun.

I dreamt of them almost every night and the word camel popped up everywhere. I'd pass two old ladies chatting over trolleys at the supermarket, their conversation a muted blur, then radiant and clear the word camel would leap out. As I sat watching the weather report on TV, I was convinced that amid the raised dust and endless heat the word camel had been mentioned. When I sat quietly on our veranda at night I could hear the camels soft-bellied moans so similar to the call of the whales being carried in on the wind. It was happening for Gill too, subliminally camels had invaded our lives and neither of us could stop thinking about them!

When Adi offered us Kunkaa a few weeks later, I was unexpectedly delighted, although a little surprised. I thought Adi had given up on me completely and I felt honoured she'd entrust her little calf to us. Kunkaa means crow in Pitjantjatjara aboriginal language and even if I didn't yet have an affinity with the camel, I definitely had one with the crow. She arrived on the same day as Jianti, another young camel cow we bought for $300, just so that Kunkaa would have a friend.

How innocently I welcomed them. How easily they wooed me with their big dark eyes, long lashes and their charming and adorable ways. I didn't just fall in love - I dived in, naked and bare. When I was with the camels I knew I was exactly where I was meant to be, nothing else existed. The normal mundane stresses of life, bills and obligations faded into a past life. If I had known then what I'd have to let go off to keep them in my life, I don't know if I would have been brave enough to let them in. I might have kept the gate firmly closed, but it's often the most unexpected journeys that yield the greatest treasure.

I know that now, but I didn't then.

Chapter One from Kye's Book 'Love We Live' about her extraordinary journey with fifty rescued animals.

Two people, fifty rescued animals, and a journey through Australia's most challenging terrain. But would dust storms, wild bull camels, and exhaustion prove too much?

Also by Kye Crow

Wild Holy Love- A true mystical adventure

Book One- Love We Live – My Leap of Faith with fifty
rescued animals

Book Two- Tracks of Love -A heartfelt Journey of Love

Sacred Journey into the Animal Realms

Sacred Journey into the Animal Realms Wisdom Cards
– 55 gold edged cards -available only from our website

www.kyecrow.love

For up to date news please join our mailing list

www.ingramcontent.com/pod-product-compliance
Lightning Source LLC
Chambersburg PA
CBHW021857020426
42334CB00013B/365